Application for Political Asylum with Religious Asylum Application

Understanding Your Rights and the Legal Process for Religious and Political Asylum

Attorney Brian D. Lerner

LAW OFFICES OF BRIAN D. LERNER
A PROFESSIONAL CORPORATION

ATTORNEY DRAFTED IMMIGRATION PETITIONS

By

Brian D. Lerner
Attorney at Law

Disclaimer and Terms of Use:

INTRODUCTION

There are a multitude of different immigration petitions and applications. They are complex and full of requirements. Obviously it would be best to hire an immigration attorney to best prepare the petitions and applications. However, this can certainly cost thousands of dollars.

The next best option is to get a sample of the petition written by an experienced immigration attorney. The samples cost a fraction what would be charged by an immigration attorney. However, while the reader has to alter, amend and change the parts of the sample petition to reflect their actual situation, it is a fantastic roadmap for them to use. If the reader has purchased the entire petition or application, they will have real live samples of cover letters, forms, declarations, affidavits and the necessary exhibits to use. The samples come from real cases and the names of those clients have been redacted to protect the privacy of that person or corporation.

These are petitions and applications that have been drafted by an experienced immigration attorney with over 25 years of experience. Get the benefits of that experience without the costs.

ABOUT THE LAW OFFICES OF BRIAN D. LERNER

Brian D. Lerner has been a licensed attorney since 1992 and started the Law Offices of Brian D. Lerner, APC. The law practice consists of Immigration and Nationality Law and everything involved with and regarding immigration which includes citizenship, investment visas, family and employment visas, removal and deportation hearings, appeals, waivers, adjustment, consulate processing and all types of immigration and citizenship matters. Thousands of families have been reunited and/or permitted to stay in the U.S. and/or return to the U.S. because of the successful work of Immigration Attorney Brian D. Lerner.

This law office handles all types of immigration cases including family based and employment based. Immigration issues range from immigration court proceedings to trying to fix what paralegals may have done that was neither correct nor proper. Foreign nationals must have experienced lawyers admitted to practice law.

The Law Offices of Brian D. Lerner, APC handles cases arising from business visas, work permits, Green Cards, non-immigrant visas, deportation, citizenship, appeals and all areas of immigration. The Law Offices of Brian D. Lerner, APC does EB-5 Investor Visas, H-1B Specialty Occupation, L-1 Intracompany Transferee, E-2 Treaty Investor, E-1 Treaty Trader, O-1 Extraordinary Ability among others. Regarding immigrant visas for the Green Card, the firm does PERM and advanced degree PERM, Family Petitions, and ExtraordinaryAlien Petitions. In addition to affirmative petitions, the Law Firm represents people in people in deportation and removal hearings, including political asylum, withholding of removal, and convention against torture cases.

Brian D. Lerner has been certified as an expert in Immigration & Nationality Law by the California State Bar, Board of Legal Specialization since 2000 and has been recertified three times. He now passes on his decades of experience by allowing the Reader, Law Schools, Professors and other Immigration Attorneys to purchase sample petitions on every facet of Immigration Law.

TABLE OF CONTENTS

ABOUT THE POLITICAL AND RELIGIOUS ASYLUM APPLICATION

The Political and Religious Asylum Application is an Application for Asylum focused on the past persecution or fear of future persecution in the FN's home country based on one's religion, membership in a particular social group, or political opinion.

ATTORNEY COVER LETTER

Law Offices Of Brian D. Lerner

A PROFESSIONAL CORPORATION

LONG BEACH, CALIFORNIA
(562) 495-0554

QUEZON, PHILIPPINES
(011) 632-2251473

CERTIFIED SPECIALIST IN IMMIGRATION AND NATIONALITY LAW
ADMITTED TO THE U.S. SUPREME COURT

August 17, 2016

California Service Center
U.S. Citizenship and Immigration Services
24000 Avila Road, 2nd Floor, Room 2312
Laguna Niguel, CA 92677

Re: **Application: I-589, Application for Asylum and for Withholding of Removal**
       Applicant: ████████████

Dear Officer:

████████████ (hereinafter "Applicant"), through undersigned counsel, submits the following in support of his I-589, Application for Asylum and for Withholding of Removal:

Form:	Description:
G-28	Notice of Entry of Appearance As Attorney or Accredited Representative (Applicant); and
I-589	Application for Asylum and for Withholding of Removal.

Exhibit:	Description:
1.	Applicant's Declaration;
2.	Applicant's Passport and I-94;
3.	Applicant's Police Certificate;
4.	Applicant's Proof of Previous Employment in Lebanon;
5.	Pictures of Bullet Holes in Applicant's Car;
6	Picture of Bullets Found on Applicant's Doorstep;
7	Picture of Bullet Found in Applicant's Home;
8	CIA World Factbook – Lebanon;
9	Lebanon 2016 Crime & Safety Report – Overseas Security Advisory Council;
10	Lebanon 2016 Country Summary – Human Rights Watch;
11	Lebanon 2015/2016 Annual Report – Amnesty International;
12.	Lebanon Travel Warning – U.S. Department of State;
13.	Lebanon 2015 International Religious Freedom Report – U.S. Department of State.
14.	2015 Country Reports on Human Rights Practices: Lebanon – U.S. Department of State.

I.
STATEMENT OF FACTS AND PROCEDURAL HISTORY.

Applicant is a 38-year-old single male, native and citizen of ████ who last entered the United States as a B-2 nonimmigrant at ████████████ on July 6, 2016. **Exhibit 2.**

In 2010, Applicant began working for BankMed in ████ as a Housing Collection Specialist. BankMed is owned by former Prime Minister, Saad Hariri, a figurehead of the March 14 movement, a group of political parties and independents in████ formed in 2005 that are united by their anti-Syrian regime stance and their opposition to the March 8 Alliance.

Applicant is afraid of returning to ████ because of problems he has had with pro-Syrian militants in ████ as a result of his religion, political beliefs and employment. Applicant has been recruited, taken against his will and threatened in different ways as follows:

- On several occasions, Applicant's building and neighborhood was surrounded by pro-Syrian militants, including Hezbollah, questioning individuals regarding their political beliefs and attempting to draft them into the Syrian war.

- In May 2015, on his way home from work, as he passed by a cafe known to be owned/rented by pro-Syrian militants, Applicant was approached by a pro-Syrian militant in an attempt to get me to fight in Syria with them (two militants rode up on a motorcycle and one approached Applicant). Applicant explained that he was not a fighter and not into violence but was told that he was either with them or against them.

- In August 2015 when Applicant returned from a short visit to the United States, he was picked up by what he thought was a cab but ended up being two armed pro-Syrian militants. His luggage was quickly put into the trunk and he was forced into the front seat. The driver did not take the main airport road but instead went down a dirt road, while they interrogated Applicant about his whereabouts, his family, his religion and his political beliefs.

- In September 2015, Applicant was threatened by a local, well-known, pro-Syrian militant who owned a bakery near Applicant's home.

- In November 2015, Applicant heard several gun shots outside his building at night and the next morning found 4 bullet holes in his car, including one in the window.

- In January 2016, Applicant found 3 bullets on his doorstep.

- In May 2016, Applicant found a bullet in his living room.

Exhibits 1 and 4-7.

II.
ASYLUM UNDER SECTION 208 OF THE IMMIGRATION AND NATIONALITY ACT.

Pursuant to section 208(b)(1) of the Immigration and Nationality Act (hereinafter "INA" or "Act"), the Attorney General may grant asylum to any applicant who qualifies as a "refugee." The Act defines a "refugee" as:

> "any person who is outside any country of such person"s nationality or, in the case of a person having no nationality, is outside any country in which such person last habitually resided, and who is unable or unwilling to return to, and is unable or unwilling to avail himself or herself of the protection of, that country because of persecution or a well-founded fear of persecution on account of race, religion, nationality, membership in a particular social group, or political opinion."

INS v. Cardoza-Fonseca, 480 U.S. 421, 428 (1987) (quoting INA § 101(a)(42)(A)); *see also* 8 C.F.R. § 1208.13; *Baghdasaryan v. Holder*, 592 F.3d 1018, 1023 (9th Cir. 2010) (quoting INA § 101(a)(42)(A)).

A. Burden of Proof

An applicant bears the burden of establishing that he or she is eligible for asylum. 8 C.F.R. § 1208.13(a); *see also Halim v. Holder*, 590 F.3d 971, 975 (9th Cir. 2009); *Zhu v. Mukasey*, 537 F.3d 1034, 1038 (9th Cir. 2008); *Rendon v. Mukasey*, 520 F.3d 967, 973 (9th Cir. 2008); *Singh v. Gonzales*, 491 F.3d 1019, 1023-24 n. 2 (9th Cir. 2007). "An applicant alleging past persecution has the burden of establishing that (1) his treatment rises to the level of persecution; (2) the persecution was on account of one or more protected grounds; and (3) the persecution was committed by the government, or by forces that the government was unable or unwilling to control." *Baghdasaryan v. Holder, supra.*

B. Defining Persecution

The term "persecution" is not defined by the Immigration and Nationality Act. Ninth Circuit case law characterizes persecution as "an extreme concept, marked by the infliction of suffering or harm . . . in a way regarded as offensive." *Li v. Ashcroft*, 356 F.3d 1153, 1158 (9th Cir. 2004) (en banc) (internal quotation marks omitted); *see also Li v. Holder*, 559 F.3d 1096, 1107 (9th Cir. 2009). Threats of serious harm, particularly when combined with confrontation or other mistreatment and within a context of political and social turmoil or violence, may constitute persecution. *See, e.g., Mashiri v. Ashcroft*, 383 F.3d 1112, 1120-21 (9th Cir. 2004); *Kaiser v. Ashcroft*, 390 F.3d 653, 658 (9th Cir. 2004).

C. Past Persecution

Once an applicant establishes past persecution, he is a refugee eligible for a grant of asylum, and the likelihood of future persecution is a relevant factor to consider in the exercise of discretion. *See Rodriguez-Matamoros v. INS*, 86 F.3d 158, 161 (9th Cir. 1996); *Kazlauskas v. INS*, 46 F.3d 902, 905 (9th Cir. 1995); *see also* 8 C.F.R. § 1208.13(b)(1)(i)(A). "If past persecution is established, a rebuttable presumption of a well-founded fear arises, 8 C.F.R. § 1208.13(b)(1), and the burden shifts to the government to demonstrate that there has been a fundamental change in circumstances such that the applicant no longer has a well-founded fear." *Tawadrus v. Ashcroft*, 364 F.3d 1099, 1103 (9th Cir. 2004) (internal quotation marks omitted); *see also Ahmed v. Keisler, supra.*

D. Well-Founded Fear of Persecution

Even in the absence of past persecution, an applicant may be eligible for asylum based on a well-founded fear of future persecution. *See* 8 C.F.R. § 1208.13(b). A well-founded fear must be subjectively genuine and objectively reasonable. *See Ahmed v. Keisler, supra; Montecino v. INS*, 915 F.2d 518, 520-21 (9th Cir. 1990) (noting the importance of the applicant's subjective state of mind).

An applicant may demonstrate a well-founded fear by showing that he has been targeted for persecution. *See, e.g., Marcos v. Gonzales*, 410 F.3d 1112, 1119 (9th Cir. 2005); *Zhang v. Ashcroft*, 388 F.3d 713, 718

(9th Cir. 2004) (per curiam); *Melkonian v. Ashcroft*, 320 F.3d 1061, 1068 (9th Cir. 2003); *Lim v. INS*, 224 F.3d 929, 935 (9th Cir. 2000); *Mendoza Perez v. INS*, 902 F.2d 760, 762 (9th Cir. 1990).
Acts of violence against an applicant's family members and friends may also establish a well-founded fear of persecution. *See Korablina v. INS*, 158 F.3d 1038, 1044-45 (9th Cir. 1998); *see also Zhang v. Ashcroft, supra*; *Ingunna v. Ashcroft*, 374 F.3d 765, 769 (9th Cir. 2004) (persecution of family in Kenya); *Mgoian v. INS*, 184 F.3d 1029, 1035 n.4 (9th Cir. 1999) (violence and harassment against entire Kurdish Muslim family in Armenia); *Gonzalez v. INS*, 82 F.3d 903, 909-10 (9th Cir. 1996) (Nicaraguan family suffered violence for supporting Somoza); *Ramirez Rivas v. INS*, 899 F.2d 864, 868-69 (9th Cir. 1990) (granting relief where applicant was a member of a large politically active family that had been persecuted by Salvadoran authorities).

An applicant need not show that he or she will be singled out individually for persecution if the applicant establishes that there is a pattern or practice in his or her country ... of persecution of a group of persons similarly situated to the applicant on account of race, religion, nationality, membership in a particular social group, or political opinion. See 8 C.F.R. § 1208.13(b)(2)(iii); *see also Knezevic v. Ashcroft*, 367 F.3d 1206, 1213 (9th Cir. 2004) (evidence of a Croat pattern and practice of ethnically cleansing Bosnian Serbs); *Mgoian v. INS*, 184 F.3d 1029, 1036 (9th Cir. 1999) (pattern and practice of persecution of Kurdish Moslem intelligentsia in Armenia).

In the Ninth Circuit, a member of a "disfavored group" that is not subject to a pattern or practice of persecution may also demonstrate a well-founded fear. *See Kotasz v. INS*, 31 F.3d 847, 853-54 (9th Cir. 1994) (opponents of the Hungarian Communist Regime); *Tampubolon v. Holder*, 610 F.3d 1056, 1060 (9th Cir. 2010) (Christian Indonesians); *Ahmed v. Keisler*, 504 F.3d 1183, 1191 (9th Cir. 2007) (Bihari in Bangladesh); *Sael v. Ashcroft*, 386 F.3d 922, 927 (9th Cir. 2004) (Indonesia's ethnic Chinese minority); *El Himri v. Ashcroft*, 378 F.3d 932, 937 (9th Cir. 2004) (as amended) (stateless Palestinians born in Kuwait are members of a persecuted minority); *Hoxha v. Ashcroft*, 319 F.3d 1179, 1182-83 (9th Cir. 2003) (ethnic Albanians in Kosovo); *Singh v. INS*, 94 F.3d 1353, 1359 (9th Cir. 1996) (Indo Fijians).

E.   Nexus to the Five Statutorily Protected Grounds

For applications filed on or after May 11, 2005, the REAL ID Act of 2005, Pub. L. No. 109-113, 119 Stat. 231, created a new nexus standard, requiring that an applicant establish that "race, religion, nationality, membership in a particular social group, or political opinion was or will be *at least one central reason* for persecuting the applicant." INA § 208(b)(1)(B)(i) (emphasis added).

> "[A] motive is a "central reason" if the persecutor would not have harmed the applicant if such motive did not exist. Likewise, a motive is a "central reason" if that motive, standing alone, would have led the persecutor to harm the applicant. . . . [P]ersecution may be caused by more than one central reason, and an asylum applicant need not prove which reason was dominant. Nevertheless, to demonstrate that a protected ground was "at least one central reason" for persecution, an applicant must prove that such ground was a cause of the persecutors' acts."

Parussimova v. Mukasey, 555 F.3d 734, 741 (9th Cir. 2009).

1.   Mixed-Motive Cases

A persecutor may have multiple motives for inflicting harm on an applicant. For applications filed on or after May 11, 2005, § 101(a)(3) of the REAL ID Act provides that an applicant must establish that "race, religion, nationality, membership in a particular social group, or political opinion, was or will be *at least*

███████████

one central reason for persecuting the applicant." INA § 208(b)(1)(B)(i) (emphasis added); *see also Sinha v. Holder*, 564 F.3d 1015, 1021 n.3 (9th Cir. 2009) (applying pre-REAL ID Act standard); *Parussimova v. Mukasey, supra*, ("[A] motive is a 'central reason' if the persecutor would not have harmed the applicant if such motive did not exist. Likewise, a motive is a 'central reason' if that motive, standing alone, would have led the persecutor to harm the applicant. . . . [P]ersecution may be caused by more than one central reason, and an asylum applicant need not prove which reason was dominant. Nevertheless, to demonstrate that a protected ground was 'at least one central reason' for persecution, an applicant must prove that such ground was a cause of the persecutors' acts.").

2.   The Protected Grounds

a.   Religion

Persecution on the basis of religion may assume various forms, including: prohibition of membership of a religious community, or worship in private or in public, of religious instruction, or serious measures of discrimination imposed on persons because they practice their religion or belong to a particular religious community. See Handbook on Procedures and Criteria for Determining Refugee Status, U.N. Doc. HCR/IP/4/Eng./REV.2 (ed. 1992) ("UNHCR Handbook"), para. 72. "The Universal Declaration of Human Rights and the Human Rights Covenant proclaim the right to freedom of thought, conscience, and religion, which right includes the freedom of a person to change his religion and his freedom to manifest it in public or private, in teaching, practice, worship and observance." UNHCR Handbook, para. 72.

b.   Membership In A Particular Social Group

A particular social group "implies a collection of people closely affiliated with each other, who are actuated by some common impulse or interest." *Sanchez-Trujillo v. INS*, 801 F.2d 1571, 1576-77 (9th Cir. 1986) (stating that a family is a "prototypical example" of a social group, but young working class urban males of military age are not). "[A] 'particular social group' is one united by a voluntary association, including a former association, *or* by an innate characteristic that is so fundamental to the identities or consciences of its members that members either cannot or should not be required to change it," *Hernandez-Montiel v. INS*, 225 F.3d 1084, 1092-93 (9th Cir. 2000) (Mexican gay men with female sexual identities constitute a particular social group); *see also Perdomo v. Holder*, 611 F.3d 662, 669 (9th Cir. 2010) (BIA erred in rejecting "women in Guatemala" as a cognizable social group solely based on the broad nature of the group, without assessing 'innate characteristic' analysis); UNHCR's Guidelines on International Protection: Membership of a particular social group within the context of Article 1A(2) of the 1951 Convention and/or its 1967 Protocol relating to the Status of Refugees (HCR/GIP/02/02, 7 May 2002).

c.   Political Opinion

"[A]n asylum applicant must satisfy two requirements in order to show that he was persecuted 'on account of' a political opinion. First, the applicant must show that he held (or that his persecutors believed that he held) a political opinion. Second, the applicant must show that his persecutors persecuted him (or that he faces the prospect of such persecution) *because of* his political opinion." *Navas v. INS*, 217 F.3d 646, 656 (9th Cir. 2000) (internal citation omitted); *see also Ahmed v. Keisler, supra.* "[P]olitical opinion encompasses more than electoral politics or formal political ideology or action." *Ahmed*, 504 F.3d at 1192; *see, e.g., Al-Saher v. INS*, 268 F.3d 1143, 1146 (9th Cir. 2001); *Borja v. INS*, 175 F.3d 732 (9th Cir. 1999) (en banc) (refusal to pay revolutionary tax to the NPA in the face of threats constitutes an expression of political belief), *superseded by statute on other grounds as stated by Parussimova v. Mukasey, supra.*

████████████

IV.
APPLICANT IS ELIGIBLE FOR AND ENTITLED TO ASYLUM UNDER SECTION 208 OF THE ACT.

In the present case, Applicant is afraid of returning because of problems he has had with pro-Syrian militants in ████████ as a result of his religion, political beliefs and employment. Applicant was specifically targeted because he is a Sunni Muslim and because of his anti-Syrian regime stance, which was well known to all given his 6+ year employment at BankMed in Lebanon, which is owned by former Prime Minister, Saad Hariri, a figurehead of the March 14 movement, a group of political parties and independents in Lebanon formed in 2005 that are united by their anti-Syrian regime stance and their opposition to the March 8 Alliance..

In addition to several recruitment attempts, veiled threats and a quasi-kidnapping by pro-Syrian militants, the following incident are of particular concern:

- In November 2015, Applicant heard several gun shots outside his building at night and the next morning found 4 bullet holes in his car, including one in the window.

- In January 2016, Applicant found 3 bullets on his doorstep.

- In May 2016, Applicant found a bullet in his living room.

Exhibits 1 and 4-7.

Moreover, country condition materials establish that serious human rights problems exist in ████████ including spillover violence from the crisis in Syria, torture and abuse by security forces, corruption, kidnappings, sectarian violence, and violence by known terrorist organizations such as Hezbollah, ISIS and Hamas **Exhibits 8-14.**

Therefore, Applicant has established both past persecution and a well-found fear of future persecution (both objectively and subjectively) based on evidence that he has been threatened by pro-Syrian militants in ████████ as a result of his religion, political beliefs and employment and current country conditions in

V.
CONCLUSION

Based on the forgoing, Applicant is eligible for asylum pursuant to section 208 of the Act and therefore, respectfully requests that the Service approve his I-589.

Dated: August 17, 2016

Respectfully submitted,

Brian D. Lerner
Attorney at Law

Notice of Entry of Appearance
as Attorney or Accredited Representative
Department of Homeland Security

DHS
Form G-28
OMB No. 1615-0105
Expires 03/31/2018

Part 1. Information About Attorney or Accredited Representative

1. USCIS ELIS Account Number (*if any*)

▶ [ ][ ][ ][ ][ ][ ][ ][ ][ ][ ][ ][ ]

Name and Address of Attorney or Accredited Representative

2.a. Family Name (*Last Name*) — Lerner

2.b. Given Name (*First Name*) — Brian

2.c. Middle Name — David

3.a. Street Number and Name — 3233 E Broadway

3.b. Apt. ☐ Ste. ☐ Flr. ☐ [ ]

3.c. City or Town — Long Beach

3.d. State — CA   **3.e.** ZIP Code — 90803

3.f. Province — [ ]

3.g. Postal Code — [ ]

3.h. Country — USA

4. Daytime Telephone Number — 5624950554

5. Fax Number — 5626088672

6. E-Mail Address (*if any*) — blerner@californiaimmigration.us

7. Mobile Telephone Number (*if any*) — [ ]

Part 2. Notice of Appearance as Attorney or Accredited Representative

This appearance relates to immigration matters before (*Select only one box*):

1.a. ☒ USCIS

1.b. List the form numbers
I-589

2.a. ☐ ICE

2.b. List the specific matter in which appearance is entered
[ ]

3.a. ☐ CBP

3.b. List the specific matter in which appearance is entered
[ ]

I enter my appearance as attorney or accredited representative at the request of:

4. Select only one box:

☒ Applicant   ☐ Petitioner   ☐ Requestor

☐ Respondent (ICE, CBP)

Information About Applicant, Petitioner, Requestor, or Respondent

5.a. Family Name (*Last Name*) ▮▮▮▮▮

5.b. Given Name (*First Name*) ▮▮▮▮

5.c. Middle Name [ ]

6. Name of Company or Organization (*if applicable*)
[ ]

Form G-28 05/05/16 Y

Part 2. Notice of Appearance as Attorney or Accredited Representative *(continued)*

Information About Applicant, Petitioner, Requestor, or Respondent (continued)

7. USCIS ELIS Account Number *(if any)*

    ▶

8. Alien Registration Number (A-Number) or Receipt Number

9. Daytime Telephone Number

    6618773924

10. Mobile Telephone Number *(if any)*

    6618773924

11. E-Mail Address *(if any)*

    ████████████████████████

Mailing Address of Applicant, Petitioner, Requestor, or Respondent

NOTE: Provide the mailing address of the applicant, petitioner, requestor, or respondent. **Do not** provide the business mailing address of the attorney or accredited representative **unless** it serves as the safe mailing address on the application, petition, or request being filed with this Form G-28.

12.a. Street Number and Name ████████████████

12.b. Apt. ☐ Ste. ☐ Flr. ☐ ████

12.c. City or Town ████████

12.d. State ███ 12.e. ZIP Code ██████

12.f. Province

12.g. Postal Code

12.h. Country

    USA

Part 3. Eligibility Information for Attorney or Accredited Representative

Select all applicable items.

1.a. ☒ I am an attorney eligible to practice law in, and a member in good standing of, the bar of the highest courts of the following states, possessions, territories, commonwealths, or the District of Columbia. *(If you need additional space, use Part 6.)*

    Licensing Authority

    Supreme Court of California

1.b. Bar Number *(if applicable)*

    158536

1.c. Name of Law Firm

    Law Offices of Brian D. Lerner

1.d. I *(choose one)* ☒ *am not* ☐ *am*

    subject to any order of any court or administrative agency disbarring, suspending, enjoining, restraining, or otherwise restricting me in the practice of law. If you are subject to any orders, explain in the space below. *(If you need additional space, use Part 6.)*

2.a. ☐ I am an accredited representative of the following qualified nonprofit religious, charitable, social service, or similar organization established in the United States, so recognized by the Department of Justice, Board of Immigration Appeals, in accordance with 8 CFR 292.2. Provide the name of the organization and the expiration date of accreditation.

2.b. Name of Recognized Organization

2.c. Date accreditation expires

    (mm/dd/yyyy) ▶

Part 3. Eligibility Information for Attorney or Accredited Representative *(continued)*

3. ☐ I am associated with

[   ],

the attorney or accredited representative of record who previously filed Form G-28 in this case, and my appearance as an attorney or accredited representative is at his or her request.

NOTE: If you select this item, also complete **Item Numbers 1.a. - 1.b.** or **Item Numbers 2.a. - 2.c.** in **Part 3.** *(whichever is appropriate).*

4.a. ☐ I am a law student or law graduate working under the direct supervision of the attorney or accredited representative of record on this form in accordance with the requirements in 8 CFR 292.1(a)(2)(iv).

4.b. Name of Law Student or Law Graduate

[   ]

Part 4. Applicant, Petitioner, Requestor, or Respondent Consent to Representation, Contact Information, and Signature

Consent to Representation and Release of Information

1. I have requested the representation of and consented to being represented by the attorney or accredited representative named in **Part 1.** of this form. According to the Privacy Act of 1974 and DHS policy, I also consent to the disclosure to the named attorney or accredited representative of any record pertaining to me that appears in any system of records of USCIS, ICE or CBP.

When you (the applicant, petitioner, requestor, or respondent) are represented, DHS will send notices to both you and your attorney or accredited representative either through mail or electronic delivery.

DHS will also send the Form I-94, Arrival Departure Record, to you unless you select **Item Number 2.a.** in **Part 4.** All secure identity documents and Travel Documents will be sent to you (the applicant, petitioner, requestor, or respondent) at your U.S. mailing address **unless** you ask us to send your secure identity documents to your attorney of record or accredited representative.

If you do not want to receive original notices or secure identity documents directly, but would rather have such notices and documents sent to your attorney of record or accredited representative, please select **all applicable** boxes below:

2.a. ☒ I request DHS send any notice (including Form I-94) on an application, petition, or request to the U.S. business address of my attorney of record or accredited representative as listed in this form. I understand that I may change this election at any future date through written notice to DHS.

2.b. ☐ I request that DHS send any secure identity document, such as a Permanent Resident Card, Employment Authorization Document, or Travel Document, that I am approved to receive and authorized to possess, to the U.S. business address of my attorney of record or accredited representative as listed in this form or to a designated military or diplomatic address for pickup in a foreign country (if permitted). I consent to having my secure identity document sent to my attorney of record or accredited representative's U.S. business address and understand that I may request, at any future date and through written notice to DHS, that DHS send any secure identity document to me directly.

3.a. Signature of Applicant, Petitioner, Requestor, or Respondent

➡ [*Bhatti*]

3.b. Date of Signature *(mm/dd/yyyy)* ▶ [08/04/2016]

Part 5. Signature of Attorney or Accredited Representative

I have read and understand the regulations and conditions contained in 8 CFR 103.2 and 292 governing appearances and representation before the Department of Homeland Security. I declare under penalty of perjury under the laws of the United States that the information I have provided on this form is true and correct.

1. Signature of Attorney or Accredited Representative

[*B. D. L.*]

2. Signature of Law Student or Law Graduate

[   ]

3. Date of Signature *(mm/dd/yyyy)* ▶ [08/04/2016]

Part 6. Additional Information

Use the space provided below to provide additional information pertaining to **Part 3., Item Numbers 1.a. - 1.d.** or to provide your U.S. business address for purposes of receiving secure identity documents for your client (if your client has consented to your receipt of such documents under **Part 4.**)

Department of Homeland Security
U.S. Citizenship and Immigration Services

U.S. Department of Justice
Executive Office for Immigration Review

OMB No. 1615-0067; Expires 12/31/2016

I-589, Application for Asylum and for Withholding of Removal

START HERE - Type or print in black ink. See the Instructions for information about eligibility and how to complete and file this application. There is NO filing fee for this application.

NOTE: Check this box if you also want to apply for withholding of removal under the Convention Against Torture. ☒

Part A.I. Information About You

1. Alien Registration Number(s) (A-Number) *(if any)*	2. U.S. Social Security Number *(if any)* N/A	
3. Complete Last Name ▓▓▓▓	**4. First Name** ▓▓▓▓	**5. Middle Name**

6. What other names have you used *(include maiden name and aliases)?*
N/A

7. Residence in the U.S. *(where you physically reside)*

Street Number and Name ▓▓▓▓			Apt. Number
City ▓▓▓▓	State ▓▓▓	Zip Code ▓▓▓	Telephone Number ▓▓▓▓

8. Mailing Address in the U.S. *(if different than the address in Item Number 7)*

In Care Of *(if applicable):*	Telephone Number
Street Number and Name	Apt. Number
City	State	Zip Code

9. Gender: ☒ Male ☐ Female	10. Marital Status: ☒ Single ☐ Married ☐ Divorced ☐ Widowed

11. Date of Birth *(mm/dd/yyyy)* 06/20/1978	12. City and Country of Birth Beirut ▓▓▓

13. Present Nationality *(Citizenship)* . . ▓▓▓	14. Nationality at Birth ▓▓▓	15. Race, Ethnic, or Tribal Group White	16. Religion Muslim

17. Check the box, a through c, that applies: a. ☒ I have never been in Immigration Court proceedings.

b. ☐ I am now in Immigration Court proceedings.   c. ☐ I am not now in Immigration Court proceedings, but I have been in the past.

18. Complete 18 a through c.

a. When did you last leave your country? *(mm/dd/yyyy)* 07/06/2016   b. What is your current I-94 Number, if any? 15999159040

c. List each entry into the U.S. beginning with your most recent entry. List date *(mm/dd/yyyy)*, place, and your status for each entry. *(Attach additional sheets as needed.)*

Date 07/06/2016	Place ▓▓▓	Status B-2	Date Status Expires 01/01/2017
Date 08/12/2015	Place ▓▓▓	Status B-2	
Date 10/10/2006	Place ▓▓▓	Status H-2B	

19. What country issued your last passport or travel document? Lebanon	20. Passport Number RL3586984	21. Expiration Date *(mm/dd/yyyy)* 04/02/2021
	Travel Document Number	

22. What is your native language *(include dialect, if applicable)?* Arabic	23. Are you fluent in English? ☒ Yes ☐ No	24. What other languages do you speak fluently? N/A

For EOIR use only.	For USCIS use only.	Action: Interview Date: _____ Asylum Officer ID#: _____	Decision: Approval Date: _____ Denial Date: _____ Referral Date: _____

Part A.II. Information About Your Spouse and Children

Your spouse ☒ I am not married. (Skip to **Your Children** below.)

1. Alien Registration Number (A-Number) (if any)	2. Passport/ID Card Number (if any)	3. Date of Birth (mm/dd/yyyy)	4. U.S. Social Security Number (if any)
5. Complete Last Name	**6. First Name**	**7. Middle Name**	**8. Maiden Name**
9. Date of Marriage (mm/dd/yyyy)	**10. Place of Marriage**	**11. City and Country of Birth**	
12. Nationality (Citizenship)	**13. Race, Ethnic, or Tribal Group**		**14. Gender** ☐ Male ☐ Female

15. Is this person in the U.S.?
☐ Yes (Complete Blocks 16 to 24.)   ☐ No (Specify location):

16. Place of last entry into the U.S.	17. Date of last entry into the U.S. (mm/dd/yyyy)	18. I-94 Number (if any)	19. Status when last admitted (Visa type, if any)
20. What is your spouse's current status?	**21.** What is the expiration date of his/her authorized stay, if any? (mm/dd/yyyy)	**22.** Is your spouse in Immigration Court proceedings? ☐ Yes ☐ No	**23.** If previously in the U.S., date of previous arrival (mm/dd/yyyy)

24. If in the U.S., is your spouse to be included in this application? *(Check the appropriate box.)*

☐ Yes *(Attach one photograph of your spouse in the upper right corner of Page 9 on the extra copy of the application submitted for this person.)*

☐ No

Your Children. List **all** of your children, regardless of age, location, or marital status.

☒ I do not have any children. *(Skip to Part A.III., **Information about your background.**)*

☐ I have children.   Total number of children: _____

*(**NOTE:** Use Form I-589 Supplement A or attach additional sheets of paper and documentation if you have more than four children.)*

1. Alien Registration Number (A-Number) (if any)	2. Passport/ID Card Number (if any)	3. Marital Status (Married, Single, Divorced, Widowed)	4. U.S. Social Security Number (if any)
5. Complete Last Name	**6. First Name**	**7. Middle Name**	**8. Date of Birth** (mm/dd/yyyy)
9. City and Country of Birth	**10. Nationality** (Citizenship)	**11. Race, Ethnic, or Tribal Group**	**12. Gender** ☐ Male ☐ Female

13. Is this child in the U.S. ? ☐ Yes (Complete Blocks 14 to 21.)   ☐ No (Specify location):

14. Place of last entry into the U.S.	15. Date of last entry into the U.S. (mm/dd/yyyy)	16. I-94 Number (If any)	17. Status when last admitted (Visa type, if any)
18. What is your child's current status?	**19.** What is the expiration date of his/her authorized stay, if any? (mm/dd/yyyy)	**20.** Is your child in Immigration Court proceedings? ☐ Yes ☐ No	

21. If in the U.S., is this child to be included in this application? *(Check the appropriate box.)*

☐ Yes *(Attach one photograph of your spouse in the upper right corner of Page 9 on the extra copy of the application submitted for this person.)*

☐ No

Part A.II. Information About Your Spouse and Children (Continued)

1. Alien Registration Number (A-Number) (if any)	2. Passport/ID Card Number (if any)	3. Marital Status (Married, Single, Divorced, Widowed)	4. U.S. Social Security Number (if any)
5. Complete Last Name	6. First Name	7. Middle Name	8. Date of Birth (mm/dd/yyyy)
9. City and Country of Birth	10. Nationality (Citizenship)	11. Race, Ethnic, or Tribal Group	12. Gender ☐ Male ☐ Female

13. Is this child in the U.S. ? ☐ Yes (Complete Blocks 14 to 21.)   ☐ No (Specify location):

14. Place of last entry into the U.S.	15. Date of last entry into the U.S. (mm/dd/yyyy)	16. I-94 Number (If any)	17. Status when last admitted (Visa type, if any)
18. What is your child's current status?	19. What is the expiration date of his/her authorized stay, if any? (mm/dd/yyyy)		20. Is your child in Immigration Court proceedings? ☐ Yes ☐ No

21. If in the U.S., is this child to be included in this application? (Check the appropriate box.)

☐ Yes (Attach one photograph of your spouse in the upper right corner of Page 9 on the extra copy of the application submitted for this person.)

☐ No

1. Alien Registration Number (A-Number) (if any)	2. Passport/ID Card Number (if any)	3. Marital Status (Married, Single, Divorced, Widowed)	4. U.S. Social Security Number (if any)
5. Complete Last Name	6. First Name	7. Middle Name	8. Date of Birth (mm/dd/yyyy)
9. City and Country of Birth	10. Nationality (Citizenship)	11. Race, Ethnic, or Tribal Group	12. Gender ☐ Male ☐ Female

13. Is this child in the U.S. ? ☐ Yes (Complete Blocks 14 to 21.)   ☐ No (Specify location):

14. Place of last entry into the U.S.	15. Date of last entry into the U.S. (mm/dd/yyyy)	16. I-94 Number (If any)	17. Status when last admitted (Visa type, if any)
18. What is your child's current status?	19. What is the expiration date of his/her authorized stay, if any? (mm/dd/yyyy)		20. Is your child in Immigration Court proceedings? ☐ Yes ☐ No

21. If in the U.S., is this child to be included in this application? (Check the appropriate box.)

☐ Yes (Attach one photograph of your spouse in the upper right corner of Page 9 on the extra copy of the application submitted for this person.)

☐ No

1. Alien Registration Number (A-Number) (if any)	2. Passport/ID Card Number (if any)	3. Marital Status (Married, Single, Divorced, Widowed)	4. U.S. Social Security Number (if any)
5. Complete Last Name	6. First Name	7. Middle Name	8. Date of Birth (mm/dd/yyyy)
9. City and Country of Birth	10. Nationality (Citizenship)	11. Race, Ethnic, or Tribal Group	12. Gender ☐ Male ☐ Female

13. Is this child in the U.S. ? ☐ Yes (Complete Blocks 14 to 21.)   ☐ No (Specify location):

14. Place of last entry into the U.S.	15. Date of last entry into the U.S. (mm/dd/yyyy)	16. I-94 Number (If any)	17. Status when last admitted (Visa type, if any)
18. What is your child's current status?	19. What is the expiration date of his/her authorized stay, if any? (mm/dd/yyyy)		20. Is your child in Immigration Court proceedings? ☐ Yes ☐ No

21. If in the U.S., is this child to be included in this application? (Check the appropriate box.)

☐ Yes (Attach one photograph of your spouse in the upper right corner of Page 9 on the extra copy of the application submitted for this person.)

☐ No

1. List your last address where you lived before coming to the United States. If this is not the country where you fear persecution, also list the last address in the country where you fear persecution. (List Address, City/Town, Department, Province, or State and Country.)
(NOTE: Use Form I-589 Supplement B, or additional sheets of paper, if necessary.)

Number and Street (Provide if available)	City/Town	Department, Province, or State	Country	Dates From (Mo/Yr)	To (Mo/Yr)
▮	▮	▮	▮	10 2008	07 2016

2. Provide the following information about your residences during the past 5 years. List your present address first.
(NOTE: Use Form I-589 Supplement B, or additional sheets of paper, if necessary.)

Number and Street	City/Town	Department, Province, or State	Country	Dates From (Mo/Yr)	To (Mo/Yr)
▮	Lancaster	CA	USA	07 2016	
▮	▮	▮	▮	10 2008	07 2016

3. Provide the following information about your education, beginning with the most recent.
(NOTE: Use Form I-589 Supplement B, or additional sheets of paper, if necessary.)

Name of School	Type of School	Location (Address)	Attended From (Mo/Yr)	To (Mo/Yr)
▮	University	▮	01 2000	08 2002
	High School		10 1994	06 1997
	Elementary/Junior High School		10 1980	06 1994

4. Provide the following information about your employment during the past 5 years. List your present employment first.
(NOTE: Use Form I-589 Supplement B, or additional sheets of paper, if necessary.)

Name and Address of Employer	Your Occupation	Dates From (Mo/Yr)	To (Mo/Yr)
▮	Housing Collection Specialist	04 2010	07 2016

5. Provide the following information about your parents and siblings (brothers and sisters). Check the box if the person is deceased.
(NOTE: Use Form I-589 Supplement B, or additional sheets of paper, if necessary.)

	Full Name	City/Town and Country of Birth	Current Location
Mother	▮	▮	☐ Deceased ▮
Father			☐ Deceased
Sibling			☐ Deceased
Sibling			☐ Deceased
Sibling			☐ Deceased
Sibling			☐ Deceased

Part B. Information About Your Application

(NOTE: Use Form I-589 Supplement B, or attach additional sheets of paper as needed to complete your responses to the questions contained in Part B.)

When answering the following questions about your asylum or other protection claim (withholding of removal under 241(b)(3) of the INA or withholding of removal under the Convention Against Torture), you must provide a detailed and specific account of the basis of your claim to asylum or other protection. To the best of your ability, provide specific dates, places, and descriptions about each event or action described. You must attach documents evidencing the general conditions in the country from which you are seeking asylum or other protection and the specific facts on which you are relying to support your claim. If this documentation is unavailable or you are not providing this documentation with your application, explain why in your responses to the following questions.

Refer to Instructions, Part 1: Filing Instructions, Section II, "Basis of Eligibility," Parts A - D, Section V, "Completing the Form," Part B, and Section VII, "Additional Evidence That You Should Submit," for more information on completing this section of the form.

1. Why are you applying for asylum or withholding of removal under section 241(b)(3) of the INA, or for withholding of removal under the Convention Against Torture? Check the appropriate box(es) below and then provide detailed answers to questions A and B below.

I am seeking asylum or withholding of removal based on:

☐	Race	☒	Political opinion
☒	Religion	☒	Membership in a particular social group
☐	Nationality	☒	Torture Convention

A. Have you, your family, or close friends or colleagues ever experienced harm or mistreatment or threats in the past by anyone?

☐ No   ☒ Yes

If "Yes," explain in detail:
1. What happened;
2. When the harm or mistreatment or threats occurred;
3. Who caused the harm or mistreatment or threats; and
4. Why you believe the harm or mistreatment or threats occurred.

Since early 2015 I have had problems with pro-Syrian militants in ▮▮▮▮ because of my religion, political beliefs and employment. I have been recruited, taken against my will, and threatened in different ways, including bullet holes in my car, bullets left on my doorstep and a bullet found in my home.

Please see attached declaration and supporting documents.

B. Do you fear harm or mistreatment if you return to your home country?

☐ No   ☒ Yes

If "Yes," explain in detail:
1. What harm or mistreatment you fear;
2. Who you believe would harm or mistreat you; and
3. Why you believe you would or could be harmed or mistreated.

For the reasons stated above, I fear returning to ▮▮▮▮ and fear that if I am forced to return that I will be harmed or even killed.

Please see attached declaration and supporting documents.

2. Have you or your family members ever been accused, charged, arrested, detained, interrogated, convicted and sentenced, or imprisoned in any country other than the United States?

☒ No ☐ Yes

If "Yes," explain the circumstances and reasons for the action.

3.A. Have you or your family members ever belonged to or been associated with any organizations or groups in your home country, such as, but not limited to, a political party, student group, labor union, religious organization, military or paramilitary group, civil patrol, guerrilla organization, ethnic group, human rights group, or the press or media?

☒ No ☐ Yes

If "Yes," describe for each person the level of participation, any leadership or other positions held, and the length of time you or your family members were involved in each organization or activity.

3.B. Do you or your family members continue to participate in any way in these organizations or groups?

☒ No ☐ Yes

If "Yes," describe for each person your or your family members' current level of participation, any leadership or other positions currently held, and the length of time you or your family members have been involved in each organization or group.

4. Are you afraid of being subjected to torture in your home country or any other country to which you may be returned?

☐ No ☒ Yes

If "Yes," explain why you are afraid and describe the nature of torture you fear, by whom, and why it would be inflicted.

For the reasons stated above, I fear returning to ███ and fear that if I am forced to return that I will be harmed or even killed.

Please see attached declaration and supporting documents.

Part C. Additional Information About Your Application

(NOTE: *Use Form I-589 Supplement B, or attach additional sheets of paper as needed to complete your responses to the questions contained in Part C.*)

1. Have you, your spouse, your child(ren), your parents or your siblings ever applied to the U.S. Government for refugee status, asylum, or withholding of removal?

☒ No   ☐ Yes

If "Yes," explain the decision and what happened to any status you, your spouse, your child(ren), your parents, or your siblings received as a result of that decision. Indicate whether or not you were included in a parent or spouse's application. If so, include your parent or spouse's A-number in your response. If you have been denied asylum by an immigration judge or the Board of Immigration Appeals, describe any change(s) in conditions in your country or your own personal circumstances since the date of the denial that may affect your eligibility for asylum.

2.A. After leaving the country from which you are claiming asylum, did you or your spouse or child(ren) who are now in the United States travel through or reside in any other country before entering the United States?

☐ No   ☒ Yes

2.B. Have you, your spouse, your child(ren), or other family members, such as your parents or siblings, ever applied for or received any lawful status in any country other than the one from which you are now claiming asylum?

☒ No   ☐ Yes

If "Yes" to either or both questions (2A and/or 2B), provide for each person the following: the name of each country and the length of stay, the person's status while there, the reasons for leaving, whether or not the person is entitled to return for lawful residence purposes, and whether the person applied for refugee status or for asylum while there, and if not, why he or she did not do so.

My flight from ▮▮▮▮▮▮ to the United States had a layover in Paris, France.

3. Have you, your spouse or your child(ren) ever ordered, incited, assisted or otherwise participated in causing harm or suffering to any person because of his or her race, religion, nationality, membership in a particular social group or belief in a particular political opinion?

☒ No   ☐ Yes

If "Yes," describe in detail each such incident and your own, your spouse's, or your child(ren)'s involvement.

4. After you left the country where you were harmed or fear harm, did you return to that country?

☒ No   ☐ Yes

If "Yes," describe in detail the circumstances of your visit(s) (for example, the date(s) of the trip(s), the purpose(s) of the trip(s), and the length of time you remained in that country for the visit(s).)

5. Are you filing this application more than 1 year after your last arrival in the United States?

☒ No   ☐ Yes

If "Yes," explain why you did not file within the first year after you arrived. You must be prepared to explain at your interview or hearing why you did not file your asylum application within the first year after you arrived. For guidance in answering this question, see Instructions, Part 1: Filing Instructions, Section V. "Completing the Form," Part C.

6. Have you or any member of your family included in the application ever committed any crime and/or been arrested, charged, convicted, or sentenced for any crimes in the United States?

☒ No   ☐ Yes

If "Yes," for each instance, specify in your response: what occurred and the circumstances, dates, length of sentence received, location, the duration of the detention or imprisonment, reason(s) for the detention or conviction, any formal charges that were lodged against you or your relatives included in your application, and the reason(s) for release. Attach documents referring to these incidents, if they are available, or an explanation of why documents are not available.

Part D. Your Signature

I certify, under penalty of perjury under the laws of the United States of America, that this application and the evidence submitted with it are all true and correct. Title 18, United States Code, Section 1546(a), provides in part: Whoever knowingly makes under oath, or as permitted under penalty of perjury under Section 1746 of Title 28, United States Code, knowingly subscribes as true, any false statement with respect to a material fact in any application, affidavit, or other document required by the immigration laws or regulations prescribed thereunder, or knowingly presents any such application, affidavit, or other document containing any such false statement or which fails to contain any reasonable basis in law or fact - shall be fined in accordance with this title or imprisoned for up to 25 years. I authorize the release of any information from my immigration record that U.S. Citizenship and Immigration Services (USCIS) needs to determine eligibility for the benefit I am seeking.

> Staple your photograph here or the photograph of the family member to be included on the extra copy of the application submitted for that person.

WARNING: Applicants who are in the United States illegally are subject to removal if their asylum or withholding claims are not granted by an asylum officer or an immigration judge. Any information provided in completing this application may be used as a basis for the institution of, or as evidence in, removal proceedings even if the application is later withdrawn. Applicants determined to have knowingly made a frivolous application for asylum will be permanently ineligible for any benefits under the Immigration and Nationality Act. You may not avoid a frivolous finding simply because someone advised you to provide false information in your asylum application. If filing with USCIS, unexcused failure to appear for an appointment to provide biometrics (such as fingerprints) and your biographical information within the time allowed may result in an asylum officer dismissing your asylum application or referring it to an immigration judge. Failure without good cause to provide DHS with biometrics or other biographical information while in removal proceedings may result in your application being found abandoned by the immigration judge. See sections 208(d)(5)(A) and 208(d)(6) of the INA and 8 CFR sections 208.10, 1208.10, 208.20, 1003.47(d) and 1208.20.

Print your complete name.	Write your name in your native alphabet.
▓▓▓▓▓▓▓▓▓	پرویز دوست

Did your spouse, parent, or child(ren) assist you in completing this application? ☒ No   ☐ Yes *(If "Yes," list the name and relationship.)*

(Name)	*(Relationship)*	*(Name)*	*(Relationship)*

Did someone other than your spouse, parent, or child(ren) prepare this application?   ☐ No   ☒ Yes *(If "Yes," complete Part E.)*

Asylum applicants may be represented by counsel. Have you been provided with a list of persons who may be available to assist you, at little or no cost, with your asylum claim?   ☐ No   ☒ Yes

Signature of Applicant *(The person in Part A.I.)*

[~~Bhi~~]

Sign your name so it all appears within the brackets

08/04/2016

Date *(mm/dd/yyyy)*

Part E. Declaration of Person Preparing Form, if Other Than Applicant, Spouse, Parent, or Child

I declare that I have prepared this application at the request of the person named in Part D, that the responses provided are based on all information of which I have knowledge, or which was provided to me by the applicant, and that the completed application was read to the applicant in his or her native language or a language he or she understands for verification before he or she signed the application in my presence. I am aware that the knowing placement of false information on the Form I-589 may also subject me to civil penalties under 8 U.S.C. 1324c and/or criminal penalties under 18 U.S.C. 1546(a).

Signature of Preparer	Print Complete Name of Preparer
	Brian D. Lerner

Daytime Telephone Number	Address of Preparer: Street Number and Name		
(562) 495-0554	**3233 E. Broadway**		

Apt. Number	City	State	Zip Code
	Long Beach	**CA**	**90803**

Part F. To Be Completed at Asylum Interview, if Applicable

NOTE: *You will be asked to complete this part when you appear for examination before an asylum officer of the Department of Homeland Security, U.S. Citizenship and Immigration Services (USCIS).*

I swear (affirm) that I know the contents of this application that I am signing, including the attached documents and supplements, that they are ☐ all true or ☐ not all true to the best of my knowledge and that correction(s) numbered _____ to _____ were made by me or at my request. Furthermore, I am aware that if I am determined to have knowingly made a frivolous application for asylum I will be permanently ineligible for any benefits under the Immigration and Nationality Act, and that I may not avoid a frivolous finding simply because someone advised me to provide false information in my asylum application.

Signed and sworn to before me by the above named applicant on:

_____
Signature of Applicant

_____
Date *(mm/dd/yyyy)*

_____
Write Your Name in Your Native Alphabet

_____
Signature of Asylum Officer

Part G. To Be Completed at Removal Hearing, if Applicable

NOTE: *You will be asked to complete this Part when you appear before an immigration judge of the U.S. Department of Justice, Executive Office for Immigration Review (EOIR), for a hearing.*

I swear (affirm) that I know the contents of this application that I am signing, including the attached documents and supplements, that they are ☐ all true or ☐ not all true to the best of my knowledge and that correction(s) numbered _____ to _____ were made by me or at my request. Furthermore, I am aware that if I am determined to have knowingly made a frivolous application for asylum I will be permanently ineligible for any benefits under the Immigration and Nationality Act, and that I may not avoid a frivolous finding simply because someone advised me to provide false information in my asylum application.

Signed and sworn to before me by the above named applicant on:

_____
Signature of Applicant

_____
Date *(mm/dd/yyyy)*

_____
Write Your Name in Your Native Alphabet

_____
Signature of Immigration Judge

EXHIBITS

EXHIBIT '1':
Applicant's Declaration

DECLARATION OF BASSEL FARROUKH

I, ██████████ declare under penalty or perjury that, if called upon to do so, I would and could testify competently to the facts in this declaration, as they are within my personal knowledge:

1. I was born on June 20, 1978 in ████████████

2. I last entered the United States as a visitor on July 6, 2016, as visitor.

3. After I graduated high school in Lebanon, I transferred to Schiller International University in Dunedine, Florida, on a student visa. I graduated and then worked one year as a medical insurance coordinator at Antelope Valley Neuroscience Medical Group. In 2002, I returned to ████████

4. I worked as an Accounting and Collection Supervisor in ████████ until the summer of 2006, when the war started and I decided to return to the U.S. to again work for ████████ Valley Neuroscience Medical Group on a temporary work visa.

5. I returned to ████████ in 2008 and things had returned back to normal. In 2010, I began working for BankMed as a Housing Collection Specialist. BankMed is owned by former Prime Minister, Saad Hariri, a figurehead of the March 14 movement, a group of political parties and independents in ████████ formed in 2005 that are united by their anti-Syrian regime stance and their opposition to the March 8 Alliance.

6. Fighting from the Syrian Civil War eventually spilled over into ████████ which also also caused more sectarian violence in ████████ with many of Sunni Muslims.

7. Unfortunately, the pro-Syrian regime has a strong military hold across Lebanon, including the capital of Beirut where I lived, and they started drafting young muslim men to fight in Syria, and anyone who was against them or refused was assaulted or threatened.

8. On several occasions, our building and neighborhood was surrounded by pro-Syrian militants, including Hezbollah, questioning individuals regarding their political beliefs and attempting to draft them into the Syrian war.

9. In May 2015, on my way home from work as I passed by a cafe known to be owned/rented by pro-Syrian militants, I was approached by a pro-Syrian militant in an attempt to get me to fight in Syria with them (two militants rode up on a motorcycle and one approached me). I explained to him that I was not a fighter and not into violence but he said I was either with them or against them them.

10. In August 2015 when I returned from a short visit to the U.S., I was picked up by what I thought was a cab but ended up being two armed pro-Syrian militants. My luggage was quickly put into the trunk and I was forced into the front seat. They did not take the main airport road but instead went down a dirt road, while they interrogated me about my

whereabouts, my family, my religion and my political beliefs. It was clear that they knew who I was, knew who I worked for and knew about my anti-Syrian regime stance. Luckily, I was able to bribe the driver with $200 (a normal taxi would have only cost about $20) and I was taken home with no other problems.

11. In September 2015, I was also threatened by a local, well-known, pro-Syrian militant who owned a bakery near our home.

12. In November 2015, I heard several gun shots outside our building at night and the next morning found 4 bullet holes in my car, including one in the window.

13. In January 2016, I found 3 bullets on our doorstep on my way to work, a clear threat.

14. Finally, in May 2016, I found a bullet in our living room.

15. It is clear that all these incidents were a result of my employment and anti-Syrian regime stance. However, I never reported any these incidents because it would have put my entire family at risk and I know there was no way for the government to protect me.

16. In July 2016, I returned to the United States. I am afraid to return to Lebanon as it is only a matter of time that these pro-Syrian militants follow through on their threats. For these reasons, I pray that Immigration grant my asylum application.

I certify under penalty of perjury, under the laws of the United States of America, that the above statements are true and correct to the best of my knowledge and ability. Executed in Lancaster, California.

_____   _8/15/2016_
                                                     Date

REPUBLIQUE LIBANAISE
PASSEPORT

Profession

ولي صاحب الجواز

Signature du titulaire
Signature of bearer

REPUBLIQUE LIBANAISE	الجمهورية اللبنانية	REPUBLIC OF

Nº de Passeport/Passport

RL 3586984

الأمم : باسل

جواز سفر
PASSEPORT
PASSPORT

Type Code
P LBN

الشهرة : فروخ

Prénom
First Name

الأم : سي

Num
Name

الجنسية : لبنانية

Nationalité / Nationality Libanaise / Lebanese

Lieu de Naissance **BEYROUTH**
Place of Birth

محل الولادة : بيروت

Date de naissance / Date of Birth : 20/06/78

تاريخ الولادة : ٢٠/٠٦/٧٨

Sexe / Sex : M   الجنس : ذكر

Autorité / Authority

السلطة

Date de Délivrance
Date of Issue :
05/02/16   ١٦/٠٢/٠٥

D.G.S.G
GENERAL DE DIVISION
ABBAS IBRAHIM

مدير عام الأمن العام
اللواء عباس إبراهيم

Date d'expiration
Expiry Date :
04/02/21   ٢١/٠٢/٠٤

صالح لغاية :

```
P<LBNFARROUKH<<BASSEL<<<<<<<<<<<<<<<<<<<<<<<<<
3586984<<9LBN7806201M2102045910042<<<<<<<<02
```

VISAS / التأشيرات

١٣

VISAS / التأشيرات

JUL VISAS
JAN 0 1 2016
JAN 0 1 2017

38

12

الإسم
Prénom
Given name

الشهرة
Nom
Surname

تاريخ الولادة
Date de naissance
Date of birth

محل(ات) الولادة
Lieu(x) de
naissance

صورة
٣ × ٤
Photo

الإسم
Prénom
Given name

الشهرة
Nom
Surname

تاريخ الولادة
Date de naissance
Date of birth

محل(ات) الولادة
Lieu(x) de
naissance

صورة
Photo

المرافقون / ACCOMPAGNANTS

VISAS / التأشيرات

الأمن العام اللبناني
S.G. Du LIBAN
0 6. JUIL. 2016
Départ مغادرة
R.H.I.A 9183

MAYA BOULOS MISK
SWORN TRANSLATOR
Tel: 01/561995- Fax: 01/563338- email: dimisko@hotmail.com
Address: Beirut – Achrafieh- Salah Labaki Street- Abboud Building – Ground Floor

General Directorate of Interior Security Forces
Command of the Judicial Police
Bureau of the Judicial Records

Serial Number 399635/2016

Petition
of a Police Record Bulletin Number 2 (two)

Name: ▮▮▮   Surname: ▮▮▮▮▮

Father's Name: ▮▮▮   Mother's Full Name: ▮▮▮▮▮

Place & Date of Birth: on JUNE 20, 1978 / BEIRUT – BEIRUT – BEIRUT

Sex: Male

Number and Place of Register: 488 / BACHOURA – BEIRUT – BEIRUT

Nationality: Lebanese

In BEIRUT dated JULY 01, 2016.

The Judicial First Sergeant
ALI ZAAROUR
(Signature)

Judicial Antecedents (Bulletin Number 2)
Related to the aforementioned Person

Date of the Judgment	Court submitting the Judgment	Type of the Crime and Duration of the Penalty
		In BEIRUT dated JULY 01, 2016
	Not Convicted	
		The Lieutenant Colonel GHALEB ABOU IBRAHIM
		Head of the Office
		(Signature and Seal of the General Directorate of Interior Security Forces)

Page 1/1

Number 2399629   -16

I the Sworn Translator MAYA BOULOS MISK, certify that I am fluent in the English and Arabic languages, and the attached document is an accurate translation of the document entitled "Police Record of BASSEL FARROUKH".
Translation done on JULY 01, 2016

طلب

بيان السجل العدلي رقم ٢ (اثنين)

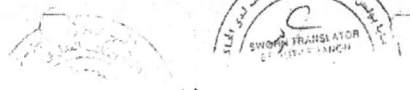

المديرية العامة لقوى الأمن الداخلي
قيادة الشرطة القضائية
مكتب السجل العدلي

الاسم باسل		الشهرة فروخ	
اسم الأب هاني		اسم الأم منى بعلبكي	
تاريخ ومحل الولادة ١٩٧٨/٦/٢٠ /بيروت-بيروت-بيروت-		الجنس ذكر	
رقم ومكان القيد ٤٨٨ /الباشورة-بيروت-بيروت-		الجنسية لبنانية	

في بيروت بتاريخ ٢٠١٦/٠٧/٠١

الرقيب اول   القضائي

علي زعرور

السوابق العدلية (بيان رقم ٢)
المتعلقة بالشخص الوارد ذكره أعلاه

تاريخ الحكم	المحكمة الصادر عنها الحكم	نوع الجرم ومدة العقوبة
		في بيروت بتاريخ ٢٠١٦/٠٧/٠١

لا حكم عليه

المقدم غالب أبو ابراهيم
رئيس المكتب

No. 2399629   -16

EXHIBIT '4':
Applicant's Proof of Previous Employment in Lebanon

bankmed

مجمــــوعة البحر المتوســــط

Capital 667,900,000,000 Lebanese pounds fully paid
C.R. 5261 Beirut - Banks list 22 - Tax Number 2641
Member of the Association of Banks in Lebanon

DP/701/2016
09/06/2016

**The Internal Revenue Service of the United States
of America Federal Government**

Dear Sirs,

This is to introduce you ███████████ who is member of our staff since 12-04-2010 and still.

███████████ is occupying the function of "Specialist, Housing Collection".

The total basic salary and the income tax of ███████████ for the year 2015 are detailed as follows:

Basic Salary	**Income Tax**
L.L. 29,120,000	L.L. 980,150

This certificate is given to ███████████ upon his request without any responsibility from our part.

Truly yours,

Mary Bardawil

bankmed

Dania Kaakani
Division Head, Human Resources

Mary Bardawil

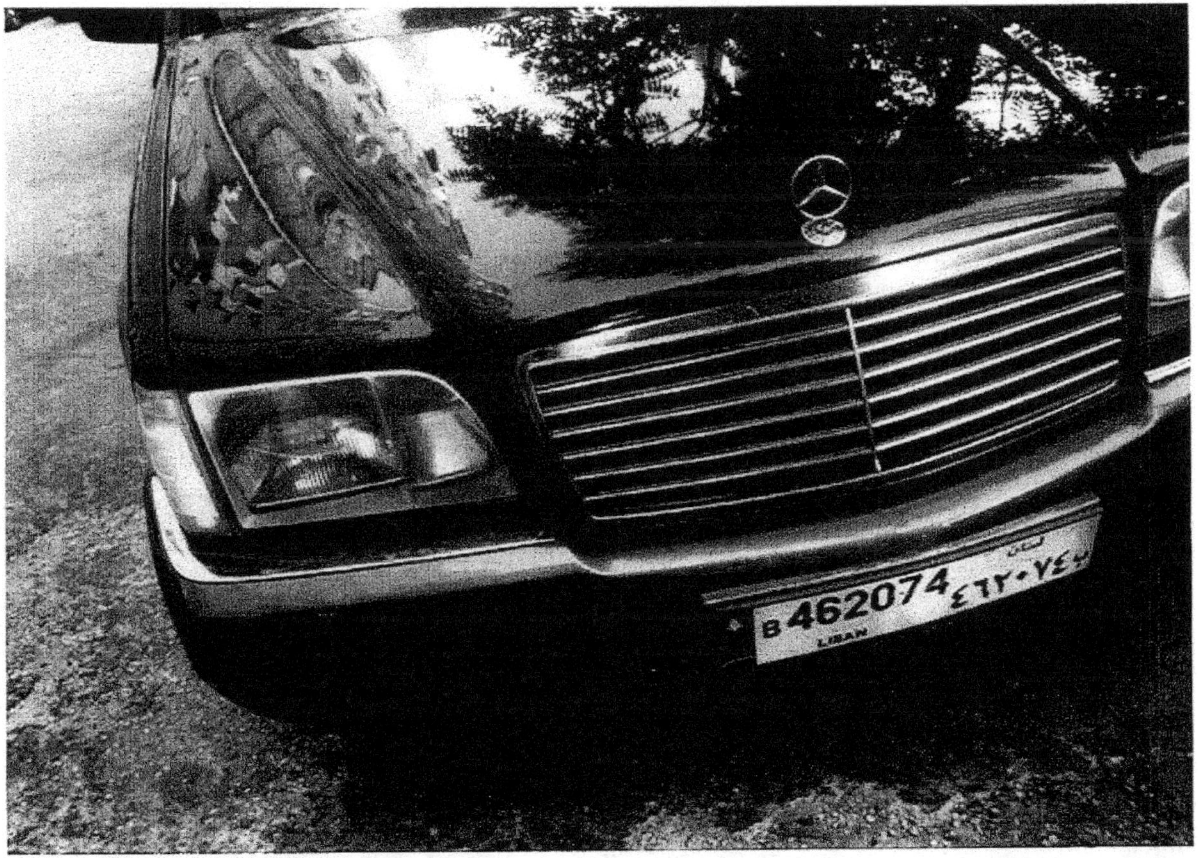
B 462074
LIBAN

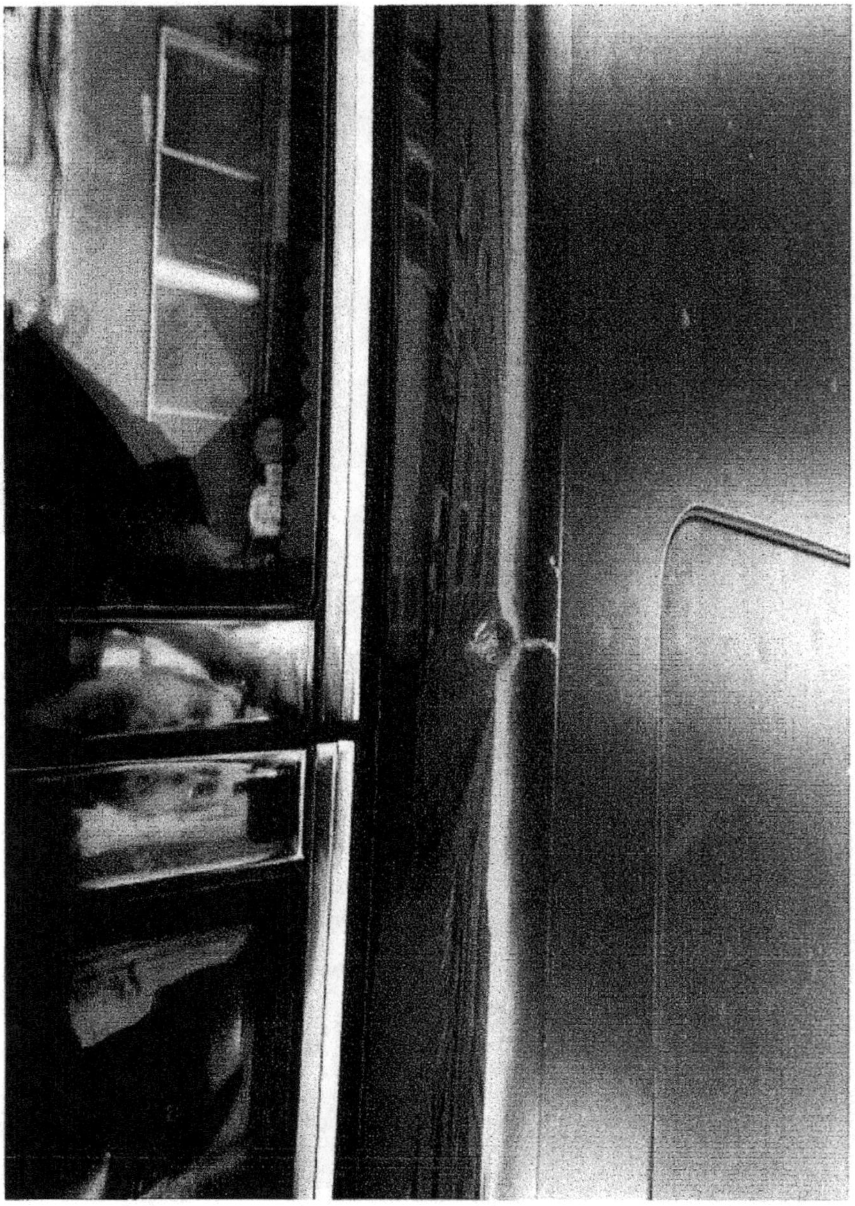

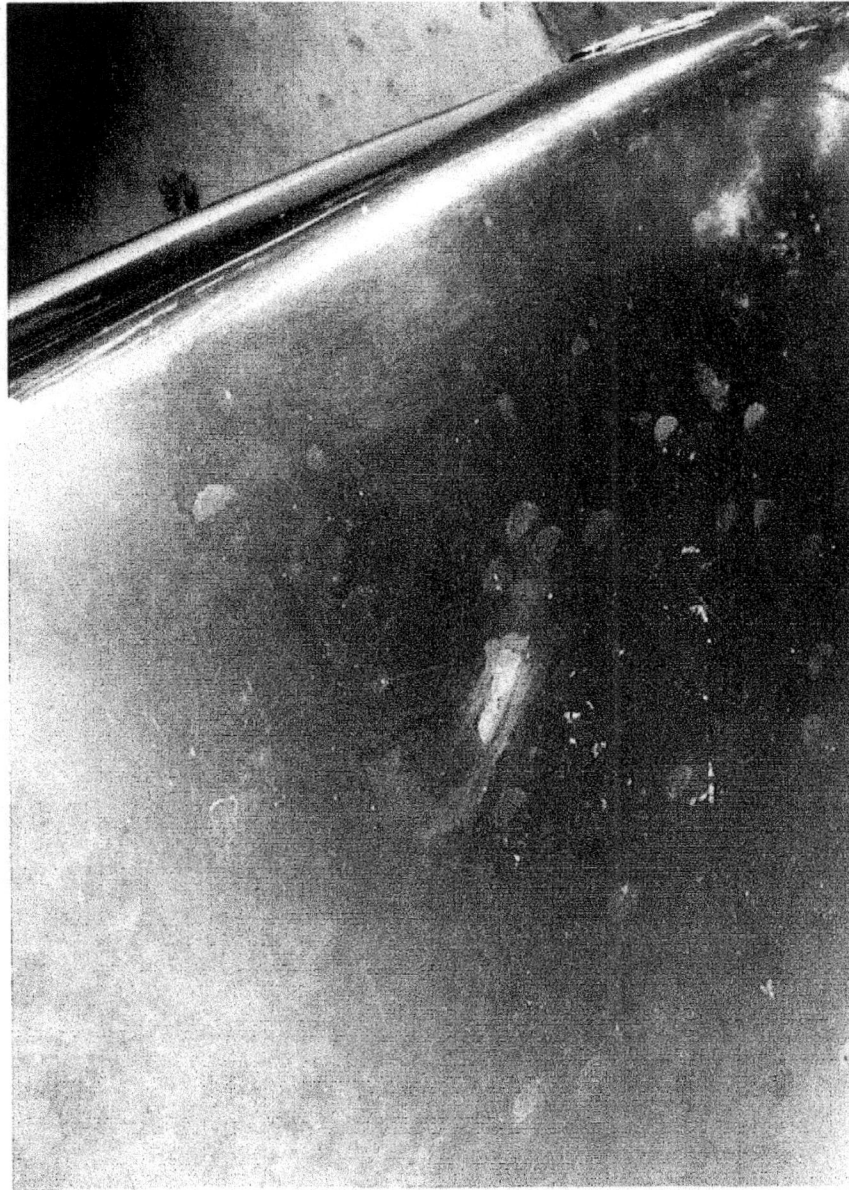

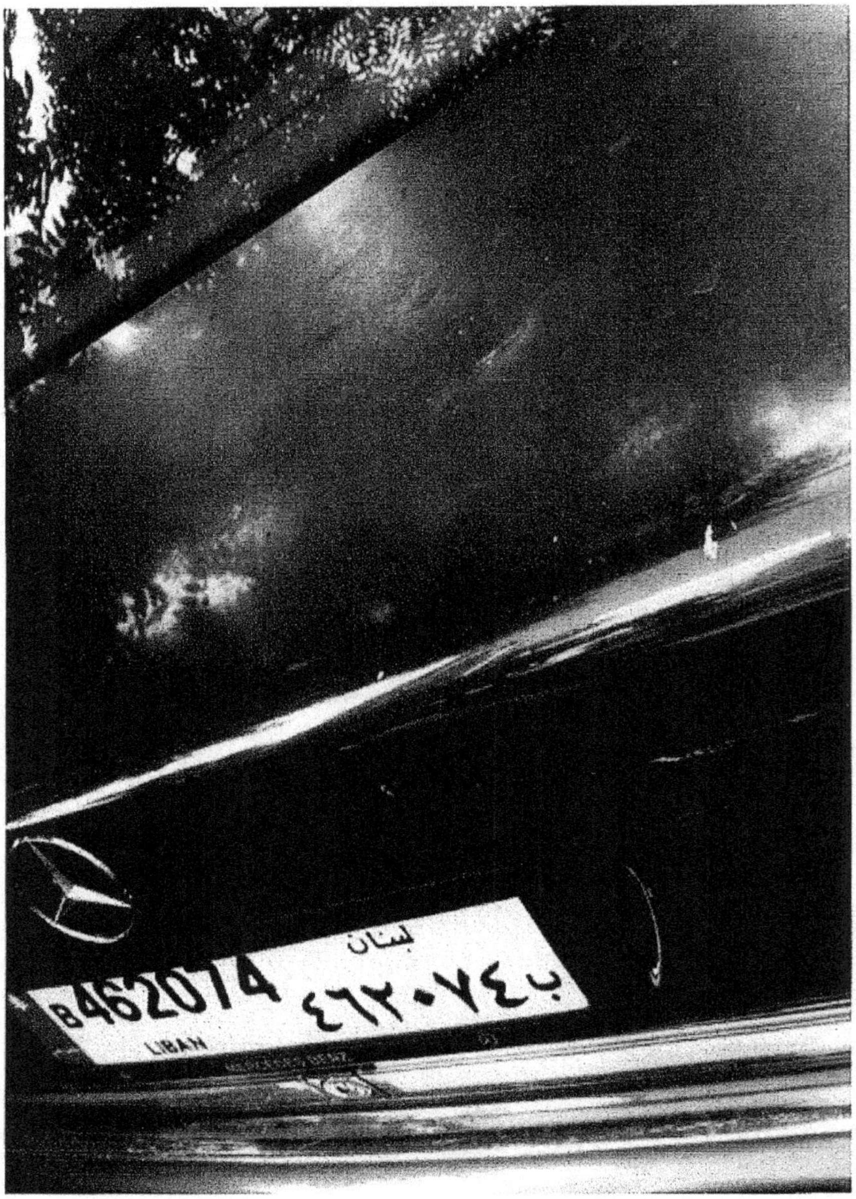

لبنان
B462074
ب٧٤٠٢٦٤
LIBAN

الجمهورية اللبنانية
٢٠٠٩/٠٥/١٦ وزارة الداخلية والبلديات
هيئة إدارة السير والآليات والمركبات
مصلحة تسجيل السيارات والآليات

رقم التسجيل ٤٦٢٠٧٤ ب

إسم وشهرة المالك ناسل هاني فروخ

محل الإقامة بيروت مار الياس شارع عثمان بن عفان بناية النجاح ط٢

تاريخ الملكية ٢٠٠٩/٠٥/١٦

تاريخ وضعها في السير لأول مرة ٢٠٠٠   خصوصية

أوصاف المركبة الآلية

الماركة	مرسيدس	عدد الأسطوانات ٦
تاريخ الصنع	١٩٩٢	عدد المقاعد ٤
طرازها	300 SE	عدد إطارات السيارة ١
شكلها	-----	وزنها الفارغ
نوعها	سياحة خصوصي	وزنها الإجمالي
درجة إستعمالها		حمولة الإطارات
قوة المحرك	٣١ بنزين	علامة الضريبة
لونها	اسود معدني	
رقم المحرك	10499012037119	
رقم الهيكل	WDB1400321A086528	

رئيس مجلس الإدارة
المدير العام
المهندس فرج الله سرور

EXHIBIT '6':
Pictures of Bullet Found on Applicant's Doorstep

JANUARY 2016
FOUND ON OUR DOORSTEPS

EXHIBIT '7':
Picture of Bullet Found in Applicant's Home

THE WORLD FACTBOOK

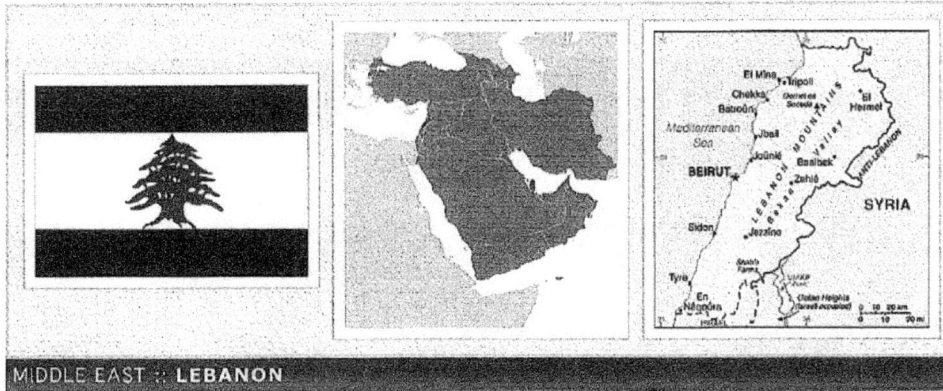

Introduction :: LEBANON

Background:

Following World War I, France acquired a mandate over the northern portion of the former Ottoman Empire province of Syria. The French demarcated the region of Lebanon in 1920 and granted this area independence in 1943. Since independence the country has been marked by periods of political turmoil interspersed with prosperity built on its position as a regional center for finance and trade. The country's 1975-90 civil war that resulted in an estimated 120,000 fatalities, was followed by years of social and political instability. Sectarianism is a key element of Lebanese political life. Neighboring Syria has historically influenced Lebanon's foreign policy and internal policies, and its military occupied Lebanon from 1976 until 2005. The Lebanon-based Hizballah militia and Israel continued attacks and counterattacks against each other after Syria's withdrawal, and fought a brief war in 2006. Lebanon's borders with Syria and Israel remain unresolved.

Geography ::

Location:

Middle East, bordering the Mediterranean Sea, between Israel and Syria

Geographic coordinates:

33 50 N, 35 50 E

Map references:

Middle East

Area:

total: 10,400 sq km

land: 10,230 sq km

water: 170 sq km

country comparison to the world: 170

Area - comparative:

about one-third the size of Maryland

Land boundaries:

total: 484 km

border countries (2): Israel 81 km, Syria 403 km

Coastline:

225 km

Maritime claims:

territorial sea: 12 nm
Climate:
Mediterranean; mild to cool, wet winters with hot, dry summers; the Lebanon Mountains experience heavy winter snows
Terrain:
narrow coastal plain; El Beqaa (Bekaa Valley) separates Lebanon and Anti-Lebanon Mountains
Elevation:
mean elevation: 1,250 m
elevation extremes: lowest point: Mediterranean Sea 0 m
highest point: Qornet es Saouda 3,088 m
Natural resources:
limestone, iron ore, salt, water-surplus state in a water-deficit region, arable land
Land use:
agricultural land: 63.3%
arable land 11.9%; permanent crops 12.3%; permanent pasture 39.1%
forest: 13.4%
other: 23.3% (2011 est.)
Irrigated land:
1,040 sq km (2012)
Total renewable water resources:
4.5 cu km (2011)
Freshwater withdrawal (domestic/industrial/agricultural):
total: 1.31 cu km/yr (29%/11%/60%)
per capita: 316.8 cu m/yr (2005)
Natural hazards:
dust storms, sandstorms
Environment - current issues:
deforestation; soil erosion; desertification; air pollution in Beirut from vehicular traffic and the burning of industrial wastes; pollution of coastal waters from raw sewage and oil spills
Environment - international agreements:
party to: Biodiversity, Climate Change, Climate Change-Kyoto Protocol, Desertification, Hazardous Wastes, Law of the Sea, Ozone Layer Protection, Ship Pollution, Wetlands
signed, but not ratified: Environmental Modification, Marine Life Conservation
Geography - note:
smallest country in continental Asia; Nahr el Litani is the only major river in Near East not crossing an international boundary; rugged terrain historically helped isolate, protect, and develop numerous factional groups based on religion, clan, and ethnicity

People and Society :: ██████

Nationality:
noun: Lebanese (singular and plural)
adjective: Lebanese
Ethnic groups:
Arab 95%, Armenian 4%, other 1%
note: many Christian Lebanese do not identify themselves as Arab but rather as descendents of the ancient Canaanites and prefer to be called Phoenicians
Languages:
Arabic (official), French, English, Armenian
Religions:
Muslim 54% (27% Sunni, 27% Shia), Christian 40.5% (includes 21% Maronite Catholic, 8% Greek Orthodox, 5% Greek Catholic, 6.5% other Christian), Druze 5.6%, very small numbers of Jews, Baha'is, Buddhists, Hindus, and Mormons
note: 18 religious sects recognized (2012 est.)
Population:
6,184,701 (July 2015 est.)
country comparison to the world: 109

Age structure:
0-14 years: 25.08% (male 793,837/female 757,120)
15-24 years: 17.04% (male 539,232/female 514,394)
25-54 years: 44.13% (male 1,378,852/female 1,350,506)
55-64 years: 7.18% (male 205,933/female 237,849)
65 years and over: 6.58% (male 179,983/female 226,995) (2015 est.)
Dependency ratios:
total dependency ratio: 47.3%
youth dependency ratio: 35.4%
elderly dependency ratio: 12%
potential support ratio: 8.3% (2015 est.)
Median age:
total: 29.4 years
male: 28.8 years
female: 30 years (2015 est.)
country comparison to the world: 118
Population growth rate:
0.86% (2015 est.)
country comparison to the world: 128
Birth rate:
14.59 births/1,000 population (2015 est.)
country comparison to the world: 133
Death rate:
4.88 deaths/1,000 population (2015 est.)
country comparison to the world: 191
Net migration rate:
-1.1 migrant(s)/1,000 population (2015 est.)
country comparison to the world: 150
Urbanization:
urban population: 87.8% of total population (2015)
rate of urbanization: 3.18% annual rate of change (2010-15 est.)
Major urban areas - population:
BEIRUT (capital) 2.226 million (2015)
Sex ratio:
at birth: 1.05 male(s)/female
0-14 years: 1.05 male(s)/female
15-24 years: 1.05 male(s)/female
25-54 years: 1.02 male(s)/female
55-64 years: 0.87 male(s)/female
65 years and over: 0.79 male(s)/female
total population: 1 male(s)/female (2015 est.)
Maternal mortality rate:
15 deaths/100,000 live births (2015 est.)
country comparison to the world: 130
Infant mortality rate:
total: 7.76 deaths/1,000 live births
male: 8.18 deaths/1,000 live births
female: 7.32 deaths/1,000 live births (2015 est.)
country comparison to the world: 155
Life expectancy at birth:
total population: 77.4 years
male: 76.18 years
female: 78.69 years (2015 est.)
country comparison to the world: 70
Total fertility rate:
1.73 children born/woman (2015 est.)
country comparison to the world: 169

Health expenditures:
7.2% of GDP (2013)
country comparison to the world: 73
Physicians density:
3.2 physicians/1,000 population (2011)
Hospital bed density:
3.5 beds/1,000 population (2012)
Drinking water source:
improved:
urban: 99% of population
rural: 99% of population
total: 99% of population
unimproved:
urban: 1% of population
rural: 1% of population
total: 1% of population (2015 est.)
Sanitation facility access:
improved:
urban: 80.7% of population
rural: 80.7% of population
total: 80.7% of population
unimproved:
urban: 19.3% of population
rural: 19.3% of population
total: 19.3% of population (2015 est.)
HIV/AIDS - adult prevalence rate:
0.06% (2014 est.)
country comparison to the world: 116
HIV/AIDS - people living with HIV/AIDS:
1,800 (2014 est.)
country comparison to the world: 117
HIV/AIDS - deaths:
less than 100 (2014 est.)
country comparison to the world: 117
Obesity - adult prevalence rate:
30.8% (2014)
country comparison to the world: 40
Education expenditures:
2.6% of GDP (2013)
country comparison to the world: 162
Literacy:
definition: age 15 and over can read and write
total population: 93.9%
male: 96%
female: 91.8% (2015 est.)
School life expectancy (primary to tertiary education):
total: 12 years
male: 12 years
female: 12 years (2013)
Unemployment, youth ages 15-24:
total: 22.1%
male: 22.3%
female: 21.5% (2007 est.)
country comparison to the world: 71

Government :: █████████

Country name:
conventional long form: Lebanese Republic
conventional short form: Lebanon
local long form: Al Jumhuriyah al Lubnaniyah
local short form: Lubnan
former: Greater Lebanon
etymology: derives from the Semitic root "lbn" meaning "white" and refers to snow-capped Mount Lebanon

Government type:
parliamentary republic

Capital:
name: Beirut
geographic coordinates: 33 52 N, 35 30 E
time difference: UTC+2 (7 hours ahead of Washington, DC, during Standard Time)
daylight saving time: +1hr, begins last Sunday in March; ends last Sunday in October

Administrative divisions:
8 governorates (mohafazat, singular - mohafazah); Aakkar, Baalbek-Hermel, Beqaa, Beyrouth (Beirut), Liban-Nord (North Lebanon), Liban-Sud (South Lebanon), Mont-Liban (Mount Lebanon), Nabatiye

Independence:
22 November 1943 (from League of Nations mandate under French administration)

National holiday:
Independence Day, 22 November (1943)

Constitution:
drafted 15 May 1926, adopted 23 May 1926; amended several times, last in 2004 (2016)

Legal system:
mixed legal system of civil law based on the French civil code, Ottoman legal tradition, and religious laws covering personal status, marriage, divorce, and other family relations of the Jewish, Islamic, and Christian communities

International law organization participation:
has not submitted an ICJ jurisdiction declaration; non-party state to the ICCt

Citizenship:
citizenship by birth: no
citizenship by descent only: the father must be a citizen of Lebanon
dual citizenship recognized: yes
residency requirement for naturalization: unknown

Suffrage:
21 years of age; compulsory for all males; authorized for women at age 21 with elementary education; excludes military personnel

Executive branch:
chief of state: President (vacant); note - President Michel SULAYMAN's term expired on 25 May 2014; the prime minister and his cabinet are temporarily assuming the duties of the president; as of July 2016, the National Assembly had failed to elect a president
head of government: Prime Minister Tamam SALAM (since 6 April 2013); Deputy Prime Minister Samir MOQBIL (since 7 July 2011)
cabinet: Cabinet chosen by the prime minister in consultation with the president and National Assembly
elections/appointments: president indirectly elected by the National Assembly for a 6-year term (eligible for non-consecutive terms); first round of election held on 23 April 2014 (next to be held in 2020); prime minister and deputy prime minister appointed by the president in consultation with the National Assembly
election results: NA; note - the 13 July 2016 parliamentary vote failed to meet the required two-thirds majority vote threshold; next scheduled vote is 8 August 2016

Legislative branch:
description: unicameral National Assembly or Majlis al-Nuwab in Arabic or Assemblee Nationale in French (128 seats; members directly elected in multi-seat constituencies by majority vote; members serve 4-year terms); note - seats are apportioned among the Christian and Muslim

denominations

note: Lebanon's Constitution states the National Assembly cannot conduct regular business until it elects a president when the position is vacant

elections: last held on 7 June 2009 (next delayed due to a failure to elect a new president)

election results: percent of vote by coalition - March 8 Coalition 54.7%, March 14 Coalition 45.3%; seats by coalition - March 14 Coalition 71; March 8 Coalition 57; seats by coalition following 16 July 2012 byelection held to fill one seat - March 14 Coalition 72, March 8 Coalition 56

Judicial branch:

highest court(s): Court of Cassation or Supreme Court (organized into 4 divisions, each with a presiding judge and 2 associate judges); Constitutional Council (consists of 10 members)

judge selection and term of office: Court of Cassation judges appointed by Supreme Judicial Council, headed by the chief justice, and includes other judicial officials; judge tenure NA; Constitutional Council members appointed - 5 by the Council of Ministers and 5 by parliament; members serve 5-year terms

subordinate courts: Courts of Appeal; Courts of First Instance; specialized tribunals, religious courts; military courts

Political parties and leaders:

14 March Coalition:
Democratic Left Movement or DLM [Elias ATALLAH]
Future Movement Bloc [Sa'ad al-HARIRI]
Kata'ib Party [Sami GEMAYEL]
Lebanese Forces [Samir JA'JA]
Marada Movement [Sulayman FRANJIEH]
Social Democratic Hunchakian Party [Hagop DIKRANIAN]

8 March Coalition:
Amal Movement [Nabih BERRI]
Free Patriotic Movement [Gibran BASSIL]
Lebanese Democratic Party [Emir Talal ARSLAN]
Loyalty to the Resistance Bloc [Mohammad RA'AD] (includes Hizballah [Hassan NASRALLAH])
Marada Movement [Sulayman FRANJIEH]
Syrian Ba'th Party [Abdel Mouin GHAZI]
Syrian Social Nationalist Party [Ali QANSO]

Independent: Metn Bloc [Michel MURR]
Progressive Socialist Party or PSP [Walid JUNBLATT]
Tashnag or ARF [Hagop DHATCHERIAN]

Political pressure groups and leaders:
Maronite Church [Patriarch Bishara al-Ra'i]

note: most sects retain militias and a number of militant groups operate in Palestinian refugee camps

International organization participation:
ABEDA, AFESD, AMF, CAEU, FAO, G-24, G-77, IAEA, IBRD, ICAO, ICC (national committees), ICRM, IDA, IDB, IFAD, IFC, IFRCS, ILO, IMF, IMO, IMSO, Interpol, IOC, IPU, ISO, ITSO, ITU, LAS, MIGA, NAM, OAS (observer), OIC, OIF, OPCW, PCA, UN, UNCTAD, UNESCO, UNHCR, UNIDO, UNRWA, UNWTO, UPU, WCO, WFTU (NGOs), WHO, WIPO, WMO, WTO (observer)

Diplomatic representation in the US:

chief of mission: Ambassador (vacant); Charge d'Affaries Carla JAZZAR (since 28 January 2016)

chancery: 2560 28th Street NW, Washington, DC 20008

telephone: [1] (202) 939-6300

FAX: [1] (202) 939-6324

consulate(s) general: Detroit, New York, Los Angeles

Diplomatic representation from the US:

chief of mission: Ambassador Elizabeth H. RICHARD (since May 2016)

embassy: Awkar, Lebanon (Awkar facing the Municipality)

mailing address: P. O. Box 70-840, Antelias, Lebanon; from US: US Embassy Beirut, 6070 Beirut Place, Washington, DC 20521-6070

telephone: [961] (4) 542600, 543600
FAX: [961] (4) 544136
Flag description:
three horizontal bands consisting of red (top), white (middle, double width), and red (bottom) with a green cedar tree centered in the white band; the red bands symbolize blood shed for liberation, the white band denotes peace, the snow of the mountains, and purity; the green cedar tree is the symbol of Lebanon and represents eternity, steadiness, happiness, and prosperity
National symbol(s):
cedar tree; national colors: red, white, green
National anthem:
name: "Kulluna lil-watan" (All Of Us, For Our Country!)
lyrics/music: Rachid NAKHLE/Wadih SABRA
note: adopted 1927; chosen following a nationwide competition

Economy :: ████████

Economy - overview:
████████ has a free-market economy and a strong laissez-faire commercial tradition. The government does not restrict foreign investment; however, the investment climate suffers from red tape, corruption, arbitrary licensing decisions, complex customs procedures, high taxes, tariffs, and fees, archaic legislation, and weak intellectual property rights. The Lebanese economy is service-oriented; main growth sectors include banking and tourism.

The 1975-90 civil war seriously damaged Lebanon's economic infrastructure, cut national output by half, and derailed Lebanon's position as a Middle Eastern entrepot and banking hub. Following the civil war, Lebanon rebuilt much of its war-torn physical and financial infrastructure by borrowing heavily, mostly from domestic banks, which saddled the government with a huge debt burden. Pledges of economic and financial reforms made at separate international donor conferences during the 2000s have mostly gone unfulfilled, including those made during the Paris III Donor Conference in 2007, following the July 2006 war.

Spillover from the Syrian conflict, including the influx of more than 1.1 million registered Syrian refugees, has increased internal tension and slowed economic growth to the 1-2% range in 2011-15, after four years of averaging 8% growth. Syrian refugees have increased the labor supply, but pushed more Lebanese into unemployment. Chronic fiscal deficits have increased Lebanon's debt-to-GDP ratio, the fourth highest in the world; most of the debt is held internally by Lebanese banks. Weak economic growth limits tax revenues, while the largest government expenditures remain debt servicing, salaries for government workers, and transfers to the electricity sector. These limitations constrain other government spending and limit the government's ability to invest in necessary infrastructure improvements, such as water, electricity, and transportation.

GDP (purchasing power parity):
$83.06 billion (2015 est.)
$82.23 billion (2014 est.)
$80.62 billion (2013 est.)
note: data are in 2015 US dollars
country comparison to the world: 88
GDP (official exchange rate):
$51.17 billion (2015 est.)
GDP - real growth rate:
1% (2015 est.)
2% (2014 est.)
2.5% (2013 est.)
country comparison to the world: 175
GDP - per capita (PPP):
$18,200 (2015 est.)
$18,200 (2014 est.)
$18,000 (2013 est.)
note: data are in 2015 US dollars
country comparison to the world: 91

Gross national saving:
-3.7% of GDP (2015 est.)
-3% of GDP (2014 est.)
-2.6% of GDP (2013 est.)
country comparison to the world: 172
GDP - composition, by end use:
household consumption: 88%
government consumption: 12.4%
investment in fixed capital: 26.1%
investment in inventories: 0.5%
exports of goods and services: 20.4%
imports of goods and services: -47.4% (2015 est.)
GDP - composition, by sector of origin:
agriculture: 5.6%
industry: 24.7%
services: 69.7% (2015 est.)
Agriculture - products:
citrus, grapes, tomatoes, apples, vegetables, potatoes, olives, tobacco; sheep, goats
Industries:
banking, tourism, food processing, wine, jewelry, cement, textiles, mineral and chemical products, wood and furniture products, oil refining, metal fabricating
Industrial production growth rate:
1.7% (2015 est.)
country comparison to the world: 126
Labor force:
1.628 million
note: does not include as many as 1 million foreign workers, nor refugees (2013 est.)
country comparison to the world: 128
Labor force - by occupation:
agriculture: NA%
industry: NA%
services: NA%
Unemployment rate:
NA%
Population below poverty line:
28.6% (2004 est.)
Household income or consumption by percentage share:
lowest 10%:   NA%
highest 10%:   NA%
Budget:
revenues: $10.28 billion
expenditures: $14.28 billion (2015 est.)
Taxes and other revenues:
20.1% of GDP (2015 est.)
country comparison to the world: 154
Budget surplus (+) or deficit (-):
-7.8% of GDP (2015 est.)
country comparison to the world: 197
Public debt:
138.8% of GDP (2015 est.)
135.4% of GDP (2014 est.)
note: data cover central government debt, and exclude debt instruments issued (or owned) by government entities other than the treasury; the data include treasury debt held by foreign entities; the data include debt issued by subnational entities, as well as intra-governmental debt; intra-governmental debt consists of treasury borrowings from surpluses in the social funds, such as for retirement, medical care, and unemployment
country comparison to the world: 4

Fiscal year:
calendar year

Inflation rate (consumer prices):
-3.7% (2015 est.)
1.9% (2014 est.)

country comparison to the world: 2

Central bank discount rate:
3.5% (31 December 2010)
10% (31 December 2009)

country comparison to the world: 100

Commercial bank prime lending rate:
7.1% (31 December 2015 est.)
7.27% (31 December 2014 est.)

country comparison to the world: 120

Stock of narrow money:
$6.085 billion (31 December 2015 est.)
$5.506 billion (31 December 2014 est.)

country comparison to the world: 93

Stock of broad money:
$52.94 billion (31 December 2015 est.)
$48.69 billion (31 December 2014 est.)

country comparison to the world: 66

Stock of domestic credit:
$96.44 billion (31 December 2015 est.)
$89.13 billion (31 December 2014 est.)

country comparison to the world: 54

Market value of publicly traded shares:
$11.22 billion (30 December 2014 est.)
$10.54 billion (30 December 2013)
$10.42 billion (28 December 2012 est.)

country comparison to the world: 72

Current account balance:
-$12.78 billion (2015 est.)
-$13.42 billion (2014 est.)

country comparison to the world: 181

Exports:
$3.475 billion (2015 est.)
$3.787 billion (2014 est.)

country comparison to the world: 126

Exports - commodities:
jewelry, base metals, chemicals, consumer goods, fruit and vegetables, tobacco, construction
minerals, electric power machinery and switchgear, textile fibers, paper

Exports - partners:
Saudi Arabia 12.4%, UAE 10.5%, Iraq 7.8%, Syria 7.3%, South Africa 4.8% (2015)

Imports:
$16.27 billion (2015 est.)
$18.99 billion (2014 est.)

country comparison to the world: 81

Imports - commodities:
petroleum products, cars, medicinal products, clothing, meat and live animals, consumer goods,
paper, textile fabrics, tobacco, electrical machinery and equipment, chemicals

Imports - partners:
China 12.7%, Italy 7.4%, US 6.2%, France 6.1%, Germany 5.6%, Greece 4.5% (2015)

Reserves of foreign exchange and gold:
$49.61 billion (31 December 2015 est.)
$50.5 billion (31 December 2014 est.)

country comparison to the world: 40

Debt - external:
$31.59 billion (31 December 2014 est.)
$32.2 billion (31 December 2013 est.)
country comparison to the world: 73
Stock of direct foreign investment - at home:
$NA
Stock of direct foreign investment - abroad:
$NA
Exchange rates:
Lebanese pounds (LBP) per US dollar -
1,507.5 (2015 est.)
1,507.5 (2014 est.)
1,507.5 (2013 est.)
1,507.5 (2012 est.)
1,507.5 (2011 est.)

Energy :: █████████████

Electricity - production:
13.99 billion kWh (2012 est.)
country comparison to the world: 87
Electricity - consumption:
12.94 billion kWh (2012 est.)
country comparison to the world: 83
Electricity - exports:
0 kWh (2013 est.)
country comparison to the world: 160
Electricity - imports:
323 million kWh (2012 est.)
country comparison to the world: 84
Electricity - installed generating capacity:
2.26 million kW (2012 est.)
country comparison to the world: 103
Electricity - from fossil fuels:
90.2% of total installed capacity (2012 est.)
country comparison to the world: 76
Electricity - from nuclear fuels:
0% of total installed capacity (2012 est.)
country comparison to the world: 126
Electricity - from hydroelectric plants:
9.8% of total installed capacity (2012 est.)
country comparison to the world: 117
Electricity - from other renewable sources:
0% of total installed capacity (2012 est.)
country comparison to the world: 193
Crude oil - production:
0 bbl/day (2014 est.)
country comparison to the world: 156
Crude oil - exports:
0 bbl/day (2012 est.)
country comparison to the world: 150
Crude oil - imports:
0 bbl/day (2012 est.)
country comparison to the world: 213
Crude oil - proved reserves:
0 bbl (1 January 2015 est.)
country comparison to the world: 155

Refined petroleum products - production:
0 bbl/day (2012 est.)
country comparison to the world: 200
Refined petroleum products - consumption:
125,000 bbl/day (2013 est.)
country comparison to the world: 73
Refined petroleum products - exports:
0 bbl/day (2012 est.)
country comparison to the world: 195
Refined petroleum products - imports:
126,600 bbl/day (2012 est.)
country comparison to the world: 45
Natural gas - production:
0 cu m (2013 est.)
country comparison to the world: 210
Natural gas - consumption:
0 cu m (2013 est.)
country comparison to the world: 163
Natural gas - exports:
0 cu m (2013 est.)
country comparison to the world: 132
Natural gas - imports:
0 cu m (2013 est.)
country comparison to the world: 91
Natural gas - proved reserves:
0 cu m (1 January 2014 est.)
country comparison to the world: 158
Carbon dioxide emissions from consumption of energy:
16.44 million Mt (2012 est.)
country comparison to the world: 89

Communications :: ▮▮▮▮▮▮

Telephones - fixed lines:
total subscriptions: 970,000
subscriptions per 100 inhabitants: 16 (July 2015 est.)
country comparison to the world: 77
Telephones - mobile cellular:
total: 4.4 million
subscriptions per 100 inhabitants: 71 (July 2015 est.)
country comparison to the world: 125
Telephone system:
general assessment: repair of the telecommunications system, severely damaged during the civil war, now complete
domestic: two mobile-cellular networks provide good service; combined fixed-line and mobile-cellular subscribership almost 90 per 100 persons
international: country code - 961; submarine cable links to Cyprus, Egypt, and Syria; satellite earth stations - 2 Intelsat (1 Indian Ocean and 1 Atlantic Ocean); coaxial cable to Syria (2015)
Broadcast media:
7 TV stations, 1 of which is state owned; more than 30 radio stations, 1 of which is state owned; satellite and cable TV services available; transmissions of at least 2 international broadcasters are accessible through partner stations (2007)
Radio broadcast stations:
AM 20, FM 30 (plus about a dozen unlicensed stations operating), shortwave 4 (2009)
Television broadcast stations:
12 (2009)
Internet country code:

.lb
Internet hosts:
64,926 (2012)
country comparison to the world: 91
Internet users:
total: 4.577 million
percent of population: 74% (July 2015 est.)
country comparison to the world: 76

Transportation :: ████

Airports:
8 (2013)
country comparison to the world: 161
Airports - with paved runways:
total: 5
over 3,047 m: 1
2,438 to 3,047 m: 2
1,524 to 2,437 m: 1
under 914 m: 1 (2013)
Airports - with unpaved runways:
total: 3
914 to 1,523 m: 2
under 914 m: 1 (2013)
Heliports:
1 (2013)
Pipelines:
gas 88 km (2013)
Railways:
total: 401 km
standard gauge: 319 km 1.435-m gauge
narrow gauge: 82 km 1.050-m gauge
note: rail system unusable due to damage sustained from fighting in the 1980s and in 2006
(2008)
country comparison to the world: 120
Roadways:
total: 6,970 km (includes 170 km of expressways) (2005)
country comparison to the world: 146
Merchant marine:
total: 29
by type: bulk carrier 4, cargo 7, carrier 17, vehicle carrier 1
foreign-owned: 2 (Syria 2)
registered in other countries: 34 (Barbados 2, Cambodia 5, Comoros 2, Egypt 1, Georgia 1,
Honduras 2, Liberia 1, Malta 6, Moldova 1, Panama 2, Saint Vincent and the Grenadines 2, Sierra
Leone 2, Togo 6, unknown 1) (2010)
country comparison to the world: 85
Ports and terminals:
major seaport(s): Beirut, Tripoli
container port(s) (TEUs): Beirut (1,034,249)

Military and Security :: ████

Military branches:
Lebanese Armed Forces (LAF): Lebanese Army ((Al Jaysh al Lubnani) includes Lebanese Navy (Al
Quwwat al Bahiriyya al Lubnaniya), Lebanese Air Force (Al Quwwat al Jawwiya al Lubnaniya))
(2013)
Military service age and obligation:

17-30 years of age for voluntary military service; 18-24 years of age for officer candidates; no conscription (2013)

Military expenditures:
4.04% of GDP (2012)
4.06% of GDP (2011)
4.04% of GDP (2010)
country comparison to the world: 11

Transnational Issues :: █████████

Disputes - international:
lacking a treaty or other documentation describing the boundary, portions of the Lebanon-Syria boundary are unclear with several sections in dispute; since 2000, Lebanon has claimed Shab'a Farms area in the Israeli-occupied Golan Heights; the roughly 2,000-strong UN Interim Force in Lebanon has been in place since 1978

Refugees and internally displaced persons:
refugees (country of origin): 449,957 (Palestinian refugees) (2014); 7,234 (Iraq) (2015); 1,033,513 (Syria) (2016)
IDPs: 12,000 (2007 Lebanese security forces' destruction of Palestinian refugee camp) (2015)
stateless persons: undetermined (2014); note - tens of thousands of persons are stateless in Lebanon, including many Palestinian refugees and their descendants, Syrian Kurds denaturalized in Syria in 1962, children born to Lebanese women married to foreign or stateless men; most babies born to Syrian refugees, and Lebanese children whose births are unregistered

Trafficking in persons:
current situation: Lebanon is a source and destination country for women and children subjected to forced labor and sex trafficking and a transit point for Eastern European women and children subjected to sex trafficking in other Middle Eastern countries; women and girls from South and Southeast Asia and an increasing number from East and West Africa are recruited by agencies to work in domestic service but are subject to conditions of forced labor; under Lebanon's artiste visa program, women from Eastern Europe, North Africa, and the Dominican Republic enter Lebanon to work in the adult entertainment industry but are often forced into the sex trade; Lebanese children are reportedly forced into street begging and commercial sexual exploitation, with small numbers of Lebanese girls sex trafficked in other Arab countries; Syrian refugees are vulnerable to forced labor and prostitution
tier rating: Tier 2 Watch List - Lebanon does not fully comply with the minimum standards for the elimination of trafficking; however, it is making significant efforts to do so; in 2014, Lebanon was granted a waiver from an otherwise required downgrade to Tier 3 because its government has a written plan that, if implemented would constitute making significant efforts to bring itself into compliance with the minimum standards for the elimination of trafficking; law enforcement efforts in 2014 were uneven; the number of convicted traffickers increased, but judges lack of familiarity with anti-trafficking law meant that many offenders were not brought to justice; the government relied heavily on an NGO to identify and provide service to trafficking victims; and its lack of thoroughly implemented victim identification procedures resulted in victims continuing to be arrested, detained, and deported for crimes committed as a direct result of being trafficked (2015)

Illicit drugs:
cannabis cultivation dramatically reduced to 2,500 hectares in 2002 despite continued significant cannabis consumption; opium poppy cultivation minimal; small amounts of Latin American cocaine and Southwest Asian heroin transit country on way to European markets and for Middle Eastern consumption; money laundering of drug proceeds fuels concern that extremists are benefiting from drug trafficking

EXHIBIT '9':
Lebanon 2016 Crime & Safety Report - Overseas Security Advisory Council

UNITED STATES DEPARTMENT OF STATE

OSAC

BUREAU OF DIPLOMATIC SECURITY

Lebanon 2016 Crime & Safety Report

Travel Health and Safety; Transportation Security; Stolen Items; Kidnapping; Theft; Assault; Drug Trafficking; Religious Terrorism; Burglary; Carjacking; Murder; Anti-American sentiment; Political Violence; Assassinations; Riots/Civil Unrest; Religious Violence; Earthquakes; Tsunamis

Near East > Lebanon; Near East > Lebanon > Beirut

3/14/2016

Overall Crime and Safety Situation

Post Crime Rating: Medium

Crime Threats

The Department of State continues to advise U.S. citizens to avoid all travel to Lebanon because of security and safety concerns.

Crime remains a concern. The overall crime situation has remained consistent from 2013-2015, which may be due in part to the worsening economic situation due to the continuing violence in Syria and related developments. Low-level criminal activities (burglary, petty theft, street crimes) remain common, but previously infrequent violent crimes and automotive theft have increased. In previous years, many crimes were non-confrontational; in 2015, kidnapping for ransom, armed robberies, bank robberies, and other physical assaults

saw a slight decline in comparison to 2014 crime statistics. Vehicle thefts and vehicle break-ins are frequent and increasing with no major arrests and only a small percentage of stolen vehicles recovered. Arms and explosives are readily obtainable by both criminal elements and terrorist organizations, both of which continue to pose threats to foreign diplomatic missions in Beirut.

Criminal activity tied to drug use and narcotics distribution continued in 2014 and 2015. The numbers of reported incidences of petty theft, burglary, robbery, auto theft, carjackings, and violent assaults have remained consistent over the past two years though there has been a slight dip in these crimes in 2015. Criminal gangs are believed to be behind a high number of unsolved crimes. In 2015, there were several violent robberies that resulted in homicide. Most incidents occurred while individuals were using public transportation (shared taxis, bus services).

Most of the crimes are believed to be the result of the massive influx of Syrian refugees, as current estimates are approximately two million documented and undocumented persons, who are without jobs or homes.

There are several criminally-oriented families or clans that until recently had operated without regard to the law though enforcement action against these families continues to be uneven or difficult. These families orchestrate activities such as car theft, narcotics trafficking, and kidnappings.

Other Areas of Concern

UNITED STATES DEPARTMENT OF STATE

OSAC

BUREAU OF DIPLOMATIC SECURITY

Certain areas in Lebanon, to include the southern suburbs of Beirut, Tripoli, Baalbek, Sidon, Tyre, the Bekaa Valley, Palestinian refugee camps and vicinity, and the areas along the Lebanese-Israeli and the Lebanese-Syrian borders, are known to harbor organized criminal entities, terrorist groups, and gangs that are hostile to Americans. These areas are, or have been, considered very dangerous. A number of these areas are only nominally under the control of the government and are the de facto territory of terrorist organizations.

Unless absolutely necessary for the conduct of official business, areas within the southern suburbs of Beirut, Sidon, Tyre, North Lebanon district, Bekaa district, Southern Lebanon district, (includes UNIFIL patrolled areas), any Hizbollah-controlled region, or Palestinian refugee camps should be avoided.

Americans have been the targets of numerous terrorist attacks in Lebanon, and the threat of anti-Western terrorist activity continues to exist.

The Department of State considers the threat to U.S. government personnel in Beirut sufficiently serious to require them to live and work under strict security restrictions. Off-compound movement by official Americans are in armored vehicles with armed security personnel. All travel must be approved in advance. These practices limit, and may prevent, access by U.S. Embassy officials to certain areas of the country. Because of security concerns, unofficial travel to Lebanon by U.S. government employees and their family members is discouraged, strictly limited, and requires prior approval by the Department of State.

UNITED STATES DEPARTMENT OF STATE

OSAC

BUREAU OF DIPLOMATIC SECURITY

The threat of new conflict between Lebanon and Israel remains, as well as the threat of political assassinations by terrorist organizations, present a danger to all persons who live and work within Lebanon.

Transportation-Safety Situation

Road Safety and Road Conditions

The roadways operate unconventionally, with drivers who often maneuver aggressively and pay little regard to the traffic lights/signs. High rates of speed, erratic traffic patterns, poorly marked merges and addresses, inconsistent police enforcement, coupled with little/no enforcement make driving conditions hazardous. Outside greater Beirut, lanes are generally unmarked and may be poorly illuminated. Heavy periods of traffic congestion are most noticeable during the morning and afternoon peak rush hours and during times of inclement weather.

There is a notable lack of electronic traffic control signals, resulting in frequently erratic traffic patterns and vehicle accidents. Police rarely respond to vehicle accidents; therefore, accident reports and investigations are not usually conducted by the authorities. Insurance companies have private accident investigators who respond to accidents and may be biased toward the insured party. Parties involved in traffic accidents usually settle matters among themselves unless significant injury or material damage is involved. Emergency services are adequate.

UNITED STATES DEPARTMENT OF STATE

OSAC

BUREAU OF DIPLOMATIC SECURITY

The Interior Ministry just implemented new traffic laws, to include hands free cellphones and no texting while driving. The Interior Ministry has begun to make aggressive strides in traffic enforcement, to include increased check points and the issuance of traffic violations.

In case of a road accident, emergency numbers are 140 for the Red Cross and 125 for the emergency civil police.

Public Transportation Conditions

U.S. citizens are advised to be extremely cautious when using transport, and where possible to call for taxi service or utilize a car-for-hire service rather than flagging down passing taxis or service cars.

Terrorism Threat

Post Terrorism Rating: Critical

Local, Regional, International Terrorism Threats/Concerns

OSAC

Several designated terrorist organizations remain active. Hamas, al Nusra, al-Qa'ida, the Islamic State of Iraq and the Levant (ISIL), the Popular Front for the Liberation of Palestine (PFLP), the Popular Front for the Liberation of Palestine-General Command (PFLP-GC), Asbat al-Ansar, Fatah al-Islam (FAI), Fatah al-Intifada, Jund al-Sham, the Ziyad al-Jarrah Battalions, Palestinian Islamic Jihad, Abdullah Azzam Brigade (AAB) and several other splinter groups all operate within Lebanon's borders. Hizballah, which the U.S. has designated as a terrorist organization, is a legal entity and a political party with representation in Lebanon's cabinet and parliament.

Many transnational terrorist groups train, operate, or are based in Lebanon. Poor border security, easy access to weapons/munitions, and numerous areas of non-government control create the ideal environment for terrorist organizations to transit or prepare for operations. The Department of State remains concerned about the continued threat of terrorist attacks and other violent actions against U.S. citizens and interests in Lebanon. The Lebanese Armed Forces and Internal Security Forces routinely execute counter-terrorism operations, including several recent high profile operations against al Nusra and ISIL.

Since 2013, there have been a number of bombings in the mostly Shia neighborhoods of southern Beirut. An attack occurred on November 12, 2015, when multiple suicide bombers detonated themselves in Beirut's southern suburbs, killing over 40 people and wounding hundreds. Since the spring of 2014, authorities have become more proficient at preventing VBIED attacks in their continued effort to combat terrorism. Multiple improvised explosive devices found at various locations were neutralized by able and well-trained police Explosives Ordinance Disposal (EOD) teams.

In August 2015, the government, with Qatar as a mediator, conducted a prisoner swap with al Nusra for the release of Lebanese soldiers taken hostage in Arsal in August 2014. Hezbollah has entered into the Syrian Civil War in support of Bashar Assad's regime and continues to

UNITED STATES DEPARTMENT OF STATE

OSAC

BUREAU OF DIPLOMATIC SECURITY

send fighter to Syria. Hezbollah and pro-regime forces clashed with ISIL and al Nusra on the eastern border between Lebanon and Syria during 2015, and future clashes are anticipated.

Fatah al-Islam was involved in a deadly clash with Lebanese troops in May 2007. Many of the individuals arrested for possible involvement in this incident are still being held at the Roumieh prison. The lack of movement on their cases – no charges filed or trials held – fuels tension, demonstrations, and riots.

Anti-American/Anti-Western Sentiment

Americans have been the targets of numerous terrorist attacks, and the threat of terrorist activity continues to exist. The most recent serious attack against Americans occurred on January 15, 2008, when a U.S. Embassy vehicle was targeted in a bomb attack that killed three Lebanese bystanders. The Department of State urges U.S. citizens to avoid all travel to Lebanon because of current safety and security concerns in the Travel Warning, which was last updated December 11, 2015. The internal security policies of the U.S. Embassy may be adjusted at any time and without advance notice. These practices limit, and may prevent, access by U.S. Embassy officials to certain areas of the country.

Current information suggests that al-Qa'ida and its affiliates continue to plan terrorist attacks against U.S. persons and interest. Extremists may elect to employ various methods to attack (suicide, conventional bombings, assassinations, kidnappings). U.S. citizens who ignore the active Travel Warnings should be aware of the potential for terrorist attacks and take all necessary precautions (varying routes/times, avoiding demonstrations) to remain safe.

Political, Economic, Religious, and Ethnic Violence

Incidents of political violence and instability, as well as violent spillover from the conflict in Syria have occurred in 2015. Notably, extremist fighters travelling from Syria including members from al Nusra and ISIL continue to perform incursions into the northern Bekaa Valley that resulted in significant clashes with the Lebanese military and security forces. This resulted in the kidnapping of several members from the Internal Security Forces and Lebanese Armed Forces, who remain in captivity. Further clashes are likely. The Lebanese-Syrian border is unmarked and porous in many areas; that region has seen an increase in incursions, from foot patrols to mechanized military units, and shelling that has resulted in deaths, injuries, and retaliatory events. The conflict in Syria continues to attract violent extremists into the country and has resulted in terrorist attacks in Lebanon.

Tensions have also remained high on the Israeli border. There have been rocket attacks in the north and the Bekaa Valley.

On December 20, 2015, the Israeli Defense Forces (IDF) targeted and killed a Hezbollah commander in Syria. Hezbollah retaliated with indirect fire into northern Israel and a subsequent attack on an IDF patrol.

On July 12, 2006, Hezballah guerillas crossed into Israel, killed three Israeli soldiers, and kidnapped two others, precipitating a 34-day war with Israel. Israeli air strikes hit Hezballah positions in the south and strategic targets throughout Lebanon, and Israeli ground forces moved against Hezballah in southern Lebanon. Hezballah resisted the ground attack and fired thousands of rockets at civilian targets in Israel. By the time the war ended on August 14, 2006, an estimated 1,200 Lebanese civilians and hundreds of Hezballah fighters had died, along with 119 Israeli military and 43 Israeli civilians.

UNITED STATES DEPARTMENT OF STATE

OSAC

BUREAU OF DIPLOMATIC SECURITY

The use of assassination for political purposes has a long history in Lebanon, dating back to the killing of the first Prime Minister Riad al Solh, in 1951. During Lebanon's civil war, assassination of leading political and militia figures was prevalent. A number of figures, who were prominently known for their criticism of the Syrian government's occupation of Lebanon, were killed between 2004-2008, including former Prime Minister Rafiq Hariri in 2005. Assassinations and attempted assassinations returned to Lebanon's political scene in 2012, with attempts on leading politicians Samir Geagea and Boutros Harb, and the assassination of Brigadier General Hassan Wissam, the head of the Internal Security Forces Information Branch. In December 2013, former Minister Mohammed Shatah was assassinated in downtown Beirut. The police have made no arrests for his murder. Innocent victims and bystanders are frequently wounded or killed in the assassination attempts. Security services are often unable to bring the perpetrators of political assassinations to justice because of outside interference or fear of reprisals. The Special Tribunal for Lebanon, an international organization created to investigate and try the individuals behind the assassination of Prime Minister Hariri, is underway.

Post Political Violence Rating: Medium

Civil Unrest

The possibility of spontaneous unrest continues, resulting in interruptions with little/no warning to access to the borders, seaports, airport and main highways. Public demonstrations are extremely common and have frequently turned violent. Access to borders and ports can be interrupted by public demonstrations, which usually occur with little warning. Under such

circumstances, the ability of U.S. government personnel to reach travelers or provide emergency services may be severely limited.

Blocking roads has become a common tactic for protestors who have used burning tires and large objects to obstruct roadways. This style of protest typically lasts for a few hours to an entire day. Another method used by protestors to cause congestion is "vehicular protests" where several hundred protestors flood streets with their privately owned vehicles and drive in a parade-like fashion around densely populated neighborhoods. These "vehicular protests" were frequent in July 2015. The summer of 2015 witnessed several large-scale protests in downtown Beirut where the number of protestors reached up to 15,000. These protests were organized to show discontent with the government's handling of the "Garbage Crisis."

Hizballah has organized massive demonstrations in the southern suburbs of Beirut and in refugee camps mainly centering on political or military conflicts with Israel or other internal political issues. Demonstrations frequently feature anti-American or anti-Western sentiments, and participant numbers can range from hundreds to thousands of people.

Following the Internet release of several anti-Muslim films in the fall of 2012, civil unrest was rekindled in various parts of Lebanon. Demonstrators in Tripoli burned down a restaurant belonging to the U.S.-based chain in protest against an anti-Islamic film mocking the Prophet Muhammad. At least one person was killed and 24 were wounded in the clashes with police.

Religious/Ethnic Violence

Sectarian tensions related to the conflict in Syria continue to rise and have serious repercussions in Lebanon. The October 19, 2012, assassination in Beirut of Internal Security Forces Information Branch Chief Brigadier General Wissam Hassan, a Sunni Muslim, sparked sectarian violence that resulted in the deaths of at least 12 people. From October 2012-March 2013, there were daily protests in Tripoli and greater Beirut calling for the resignation of the previous Mikati-led government. Both foreign and Lebanese extremists are contributing to increasing sectarian violence within Lebanon, particularly in northern Lebanon and the eastern border with Syria. The Lebanese security services are committed to controlling the spillover from Syria and stopping extremists or others seeking to fuel sectarian violence in Lebanon.

Tripoli is the second largest city in Lebanon after Beirut, and with an overwhelming density of Sunni Muslims, the city is considered a traditional bastion of conservative Sunnis.

The Alawites of Lebanon are mainly located in the Jabal Mohsen neighborhood of Tripoli and have close ties with the Alawites in Syria, including the ruling Assad family. In 2012 and early 2013, dozens were killed and hundreds injured in various clashes in specific neighborhoods of Tripoli as Alawites and Sunnis were involved in heavy fighting.

In October 2014, armed gunmen opened fire in the main Souq area of Tripoli, resulting in military intervention to secure and stabilize the area.

Post-specific Concerns

UNITED STATES DEPARTMENT OF STATE

OSAC

BUREAU OF DIPLOMATIC SECURITY

Environmental Hazards

Lebanon has a history of major earthquakes that have leveled Beirut over the centuries, with the last major one happening south of Zrariyeh in the province of Tyre in 1956. The coast follows a natural fault line. Most buildings and structures are built without any consideration for earthquakes. Several experts have stated that a major earthquake (6.0+) could easily level 25 percent of Beirut.

According to a report by Discovery News channel, Lebanon lies dangerously close to a fault that could generate a catastrophic tsunami. The fault, according to Discovery News, lies just four miles off Lebanon's coast and caused a tsunami-generating earthquake in 551 A.D.

Drug-related Crimes

Lebanon had not been viewed as a major illicit drug producing or drug-transit country; however, since 2009, Lebanese security services have been undertaking a eradication effort particularly in the Bekka Valley. In 2015, the Lebanese security forces continued to struggle with eliminating the production and distribution of cannabis and opium production and routinely faced hostile and armed resistance. The illicit crop cultivation remains an attractive option for some farmers due to a lack of economically-viable alternate crops. There are signs that illicit drug refining is gaining momentum, and in 2015 Lebanese security services launched a week-long counter-drug operation in the Bekaa Valley.

Drug trafficking across the Lebanese-Syrian border continues to be a problem and is, in large part, due to the absence of effective border controls. Additionally, Lebanon is a transit country for cocaine and heroin, with Lebanese nationals operating in concert with drug traffickers from Colombia and elsewhere in South America.

Kidnapping Threat

The kidnapping of American and Western citizens has been used by extremist groups who operate in Lebanon to bolster political or international attention, and it remains a constant threat throughout the country. Additionally, gangs conducting kidnappings-for-ransom increased, and kidnappings linked to carjacking and taxi robberies have been reported.

Police Response

The U.S. government maintains excellent relations with host country law enforcement and security elements. Urgent security concerns (demonstrations) receive immediate support and coordination. Overall, police are responsive and have made significant improvements in rendering police assistance; though they may have difficulty responding to crimes based on the time of day and location. This may lead to diminished levels of service and cases going unsolved or unresolved.

How to Handle Incidents of Police Detention or Harassment

UNITED STATES DEPARTMENT OF STATE

OSAC

BUREAU OF DIPLOMATIC SECURITY

If you are arrested, make sure that every effort is made to contact the U.S. Embassy on your behalf. Although the police services do take measures to notify the Embassy in the event of an arrest of an American citizen, this may not always be the case depending on the time, place, and circumstances surrounding your arrest.

Crime Victim Assistance

If you are the victim of a crime, you should contact the local police and the U.S. Embassy. Although the investigation and prosecution of the crime are solely the responsibility of local authorities, Embassy personnel can help you to understand the local criminal justice process and to find an attorney if needed.

The local equivalent to the "911" emergency line in Lebanon is 112.

Police Emergency Numbers:

Beirut: 01/300575

Beirut ISF: 01/425250

Baabda: 05/922170

Jounieh: 09/915968

Zahleh: 08/823000

UNITED STATES DEPARTMENT OF STATE

OSAC

BUREAU OF DIPLOMATIC SECURITY

Saida: 07/727156

Tripoli: 06/430950

Beirut Emergency Police: 112

Tareek El-Jdideh/Beirut: 01/858811

Hobeiche Police Station: 01/740925

Explosive Ordnance Disposal: 01/601930/1

When Dialing from a Cell Phone:

Emergency Police Department (ISF): 999

Information Department: 120

Civil Defense (Fire and Rescue): 125

Lebanese Red Cross: 140

Ambulance Service (Red Cross headquarters): 140

Police/Security Agencies

Lebanese security services have improved their response capabilities to incidents, and the authorities continue to work to address the challenges posed by increasing criminal activity. The need for Lebanese political leaders to express support for a security response to outbreaks of political violence can delay action by security services; as a result, authorities are not always able to guarantee protection for citizens or visitors should violence erupt suddenly.

Medical Emergencies

Medical care in Beirut and the surrounding area is considered good. Many hospitals have modern equipment and well-trained physicians. Most major U.S. medical insurance is accepted, but travelers are encouraged to check with their provider as payment will still be expected at the time of service regardless. Long-term visitors are encouraged to become familiar with hospitals near their homes and places of employment.

Contact Information for Recommended Hospital/Clinics

A list of English speaking doctors and specialist can be found on the Embassy website.

American University Hospital (AUH)

Address: Makdissi Street

P.O. Box: 113-6044, Beirut

Tel: (961) 1-350000;1-340460; 1-340740;1-341310;1-354911/2;
1-865250;1-374444;1-374374

Fax: (961) 1-345325

Services Provided: Internal medicine, general surgery, heart surgery, maternity, pediatrics, urology, ophthalmology, specialized eye center, family medicine, intensive care unit, physiotherapy, blood bank, pharmacy, laboratory, and emergency services.

Hotel Dieu Hospital

Address: Adib Ishak Street

P.O. Box: 166830, Achrafieh, Beirut

Tel: (961) 1-615300;01-615400

Fax: (961) 1-615295

Services Provided: Internal medicine, general surgery, heart surgery, maternity, pediatrics, kidney transplant, bone marrow transplant, intensive care unit, physiotherapy, blood bank, pharmacy, laboratory and emergency services.

Saint George Hospital

Address: Youssef Sursock Street

P.O. Box: 166378, Achrafieh, Beirut

Tel: (961) 1-585700;01-581700;01-525700

Fax: (961) 1-582560

Services Provided: internal medicine, general surgery, heart surgery, maternity, pediatrics, intensive care unit, physiotherapy, blood bank, pharmacy, laboratory and emergency services.

Rizk Hospital

Address: Zahar St., Achrafieh

P.O. Box: 11-3288, Beirut

Tel: (961) 1-200800;01-328800

Fax: (961) 1-200348;01-200816

Services Provided: Internal medicine, surgery, maternity, pediatrics, kidney transplant, specialized eye center, intensive care unit, physiotherapy, pharmacy, laboratory and emergency services.

Makassed Hospital

Address: Ouzai St., Tarik Al-Jadida

P.O. Box: 6301, Beirut

Tel: (961) 1-630630;01-646590/1/2/3/4/5/6

Fax: (961) 1-646589

Services provided: Internal medicine, surgery, bone marrow transplant, maternity, pediatrics, intensive care unit, physiotherapy, blood bank, pharmacy, laboratory and emergency services.

Najjar Hospital

Address: Maamari Street

UNITED STATES DEPARTMENT OF STATE

OSAC

BUREAU OF DIPLOMATIC SECURITY

P.O. Box: 113, Hamra, Beirut

Tel: (961) 1-340626;01-346914(Admin)

Fax: (961) 1-343992

Services Provided: Internal medicine, surgery, maternity, pediatrics, intensive care unit, blood bank, pharmacy, laboratory and.emergency services.

Middle East Hospital

Address: Alfred Trad Street, Ramlet El-Baida

P.O. Box: 5871/14, Beirut

Tel: (961) 1-861601;01-809555

Fax: (961) 1-805572

Services Provided: Internal medicine, surgery, maternity, pediatrics, intensive care unit, physiotherapy, blood bank, pharmacy, laboratory and emergency services.

Trad Hospital and Medical Center

Address: 53 Mexico Street, Fifth Floor, Clemenceau

P.O. Box: 113-6431, Beirut

Tel: (961) 1 369494/ (961) 3 330311

Services Provided: Internal medicine, surgery, maternity, pharmacy, and laboratory services.

UNITED STATES DEPARTMENT OF STATE

OSAC

BUREAU OF DIPLOMATIC SECURITY

Fuad Khoury Hospital

Address: Maktabi Bldg., Abdelaziz Street, Hamra, Beirut

Tel: (961) 1-346282;01-346280/1;01-348811;01-742140/3/7;01-344882;01-344173

Fax: (961) 1-350208

Services Provided: Internal medicine, surgery, gynaecology, blood bank, pharmacy, laboratory and emergency services.

Barbir Hospital

Address: Fuad The First Street, Barbir

P.O.Box: 11/4302, Beirut

Tel: (961) 1-652915/6/7/8;01-631900/1;01-631000

Fax: (961) 1-631429

Services Provided: Internal medicine, surgery, maternity, pediatrics, intensive care unit, physiotherapy, blood bank, pharmacy, laboratory and emergency services.

Sahel Hospital

Address: Dargham Street, Haret Hreik

P.O.Box: 99/25, Beirut

Tel: (961) 1-858333;01-858340;03-230730(Admn)

Fax: (961) 1-840146

UNITED STATES DEPARTMENT OF STATE

OSAC

BUREAU OF DIPLOMATIC SECURITY

Services Provided: Internal medicine, general surgery, heart surgery, maternity, pediatrics, intensive care unit, physiotherapy, blood bank, pharmacy, laboratory and emergency services.

Metn

Abu-Jawdeh Hospital

Address: Jal El-Dib

P.O. Box: 60-144, Metn

Tel: (961) 4-716000;04-718000;03-619100

Fax: (961) 1-414666

Services Provided: Internal medicine, surgery, maternity, pediatrics, intensive care unit, physiotherapy, pharmacy, laboratory and emergency services.

Serhal Hospital

Address: Rabweh

P.O. Box: 70429, Metn

Tel: (961) 4-417911;04-406838;04-417910;03-203520

Fax: (961) 4-20363

Services Provided: Internal medicine, surgery, maternity, pediatrics, intensive care unit, physiotherapy, pharmacy, laboratory and emergency services.

UNITED STATES DEPARTMENT OF STATE

OSAC

BUREAU OF DIPLOMATIC SECURITY

Bhannes Medical Center

Address: Main Street, Bhannes

P.O.Box: 36/Bekfaya

Tel: (961) 4-983770/1/2/3/4/5;04-982772/3/4;04-986062/3/4/5/6

Services Provided: Internal medicine, surgery, maternity, pediatrics, intensive care unit, physiotherapy, blood bank, pharmacy, laboratory and emergency services.

St. Charles Hospital

Address: Raihanieh Street, Feyadieh

P.O.Box: 50/Baabda

Tel: (961) 5-454371/2;05-451100;05-953444;05-950953

Fax: (961) 5-455131;05-459790

Services Provided: Internal medicine, surgery, maternity, pediatrics, intensive care unit, physiotherapy, blood bank, pharmacy, laboratory and emergency services.

Sacre Coeur Hospital

Address: Brasilia Street, Baabda

P.O. Box: 116, Baabda

Tel: (961) 5-457112/3;05-453500

Services Provided: Internal medicine, surgery, maternity, pediatrics, intensive care unit,

physiotherapy, blood bank, pharmacy, laboratory and emergency services.

Chouf/Aley

Ain Wzein Hospital

Address: Ain Wzein, Chouf

Tel: (961) 5-501515/6/7;03-707048/9;05-509001/2/3/4/5/6

Fax: (961) 5-501311

Services Provided: Internal medicine, surgery, maternity, pediatrics, intensive care unit, physiotherapy, blood bank, pharmacy, laboratory and emergency services.

La Croix Sisters Hospital

Address: Deir El Kamar, Chouf

Tel: (961) 5-505625;05-505009;05-505440;05-505625

Fax: (961) 5-505678

Services Provided: Internal medicine, surgery, maternity, pediatrics, physiotherapy, laboratory and emergency services.

Al-Iman Hospital

Address: Bechara Khoury Street, Aley

P.O. Box: 50, E.N.T. Department, Baabda

UNITED STATES DEPARTMENT OF STATE

OSAC

BUREAU OF DIPLOMATIC SECURITY

Tel: (961) 5-555970;05-557038;05-554264;05-557039

Fax: (961) 5-555971;05-555562

Services Provided: Internal medicine, surgery, maternity, pediatrics, intensive care unit, physiotherapy, blood bank, pharmacy, laboratory and emergency services.

Keserwan/Jbeil

St. George Hospital

Address: George Matta Street, Ajaltoun

Tel: (961) 9-950544;09-954200/1/2/3/4/5/6/7

Fax: (961) 9-958999

Services Provided: Internal medicine, surgery, maternity, pediatrics, intensive care unit, physiotherapy, blood bank, pharmacy, laboratory and emergency services.

N.D. Liban Hospital

Address: Fuad Chehab Street

P.O. Box: 7, Jounieh

Tel: (961) 9-639040-5;09-937401-5;09-931401/2/3/4/5;09-835350/1/2;09-830989

Fax: (961) 9-831630;09-644644

UNITED STATES DEPARTMENT OF STATE

OSAC

BUREAU OF DIPLOMATIC SECURITY

Services Provided: Internal medicine, medicine, surgery, maternity, pediatrics, intensive care unit, physiotherapy, pharmacy, laboratory and emergency services.

N.D. Secours Hospital

Address: Mar Charbel Street, Jbeil

Tel: (961) 9-540480/1;09-944255

Fax: (961) 9-944483

Services Provided: Internal medicine, general surgery, heart surgery, maternity, pediatrics, intensive care unit, physiotherapy, blood bank, pharmacy, laboratory and emergency services.

Beqaa

Lebanese-French Hospital

Address: Haouch El Oumara, Zahle

Tel: (961) 8-810121/2/3/4/5/6/7;08-814451/2/3

Fax: (961) 8-814454

Services Provided: Internal medicine, surgery, maternity, pediatrics, intensive care unit, blood bank, pharmacy, laboratory and emergency services.

Khoury General Hospital

Address: Brazil Street, Zahle

Tel: (961) 8-807000/1/2;08-811180/1/2/3/4

Fax: (961) 8-804960

Services Provided: Internal medicine, general surgery, heart surgery, maternity, pediatrics, intensive care unit, physiotherapy, blood bank, pharmacy, laboratory and emergency services.

Tal-Chiha Hospital

Address: Zahle

Tel: (961) 8-807782/3/4/5;08-803609;08-802172;08-803278; 08-822165;08-806495

Fax: (961) 8-807780/1

Services Provided: Internal medicine, general surgery, heart surgery, maternity, pediatrics, intensive care unit, physiotherapy, blood bank, pharmacy, laboratory and emergency services.

Mais Hospital

Address: Beirut/Damascus Road, Chtura

Tel: (961) 8-542300/1;08-543174/5/6/7/8/9

Fax: (961) 8-543180

Services Provided: Internal medicine, surgery, maternity, pediatrics, intensive care unit, physiotherapy, blood bank, pharmacy, laboratory and emergency services.

N.D. Ferzoul Hospital

Address: Ferzoul

UNITED STATES DEPARTMENT OF STATE

OSAC

BUREAU OF DIPLOMATIC SECURITY

Tel: (961) 8-804650

Services Provided: Internal medici, surgery, maternity, pediatrics, intensive care unit, physiotherapy, blood bank, pharmacy, laboratory and emergency services.

North

Islami Hospital

Address: Azmi Street

P.O. Box: 1076, Tripoli

Tel: (961) 6-210179;06-210186

Fax: (961) 6-614437

Services Provided: Internal medicine, surgery, maternity, pediatrics, intensive care unit, physiotherapy, blood bank, pharmacy, laboratory and emergency services.

Haykal Hospital

Address: Haikalieh Street

P.O. Box: 371, Tripoli

Tel: (961) 6-411417/8/9;06-411420;06-411111

Fax: (961) 6-541455

UNITED STATES DEPARTMENT OF STATE

OSAC

BUREAU OF DIPLOMATIC SECURITY

Services Provided: Internal medicine, surgery, maternity, pediatrics, intensive care unit, physiotherapy, pharmacy, laboratory and emergency services.

Mazloum Hospital

Address: Boulevard Street, Tripoli

Tel: (961) 6-430325/6/7/8;06-431917

Fax: (961) 6-628305

Services Provided: Internal medicine, surgery, maternity, pediatrics, intensive care unit, pharmacy, and emergency services.

N.D. Zghorta Hospital

Address: Zghorta

P.O. Box: 50, Gynecology Department, Baabda

Tel: (961) 6-661204;06-660575/6

Fax: (961) 6-663800

Services Provided: Internal medicine, surgery, maternity, pediatrics, intensive care unit, pharmacy, and emergency services.

North Hospital Center

Address: Zghorta

Tel: (961) 6-664200/1/2/3/4

Fax: (961) 6-660186

Services Provided: Internal medicine, general surgery, heart surgery, maternity, pediatrics, intensive care unit, physiotherapy, blood bank, pharmacy, and emergency services.

Akkar-Rahal Center

Address: Main Street, Akkar

Tel: (961) 6-691103;06-690000;06-691100

Fax: (961) 6-691100

Services Provided: Internal medicine, general surgery, heart surgery, maternity, pediatrics, intensive care unit, physiotherapy, pharmacy, and emergency services.

South

Hammoud Hospital

Address: Iskandarani Street

P.O. Box: 652, Sidon

Tel: (961) 7-723111;07-723888;07-721021

Fax: (961) 7-725833

Services Provided: Internal medicine, general surgery, heart surgery, maternity, pediatrics, intensive care unit, physiotherapy, blood bank, pharmacy, laboratory and emergency services.

UNITED STATES DEPARTMENT OF STATE

OSAC

BUREAU OF DIPLOMATIC SECURITY

Dallaa Hospital

Address: Dallaa Street, Sidon

Tel: (961) 7-723400;07-724088

Fax: (961) 7-725044

Services Provided: Internal medicine, surgery, maternity, pediatrics, intensive care unit, physiotherapy, pharmacy, laboratory and emergency services.

Labib Medical Center

Address: Abou Zahr Street, Sidon

Tel: (961) 7-723444;07-750715/6

Fax: (961) 7-7251149

Services Provided: Internal medicine, surgery, maternity, pediatrics, intensive care unit, physiotherapy, pharmacy, laboratory and emergency services.

Jabal Amel Hospital

Address: Tyre

Tel: (961) 7-740198;07-740343;07-343852/3

Fax: (961) 7-343854

Services Provided: Internal medicine, surgery, maternity, pediatrics, intensive care unit, physiotherapy, blood bank, laboratory and emergency services.

UNITED STATES DEPARTMENT OF STATE

OSAC

BUREAU OF DIPLOMATIC SECURITY

Najm Hospital

Address: Tyre

Tel: (961) 7-741595;07-344423

Fax: (961) 7-346457

Services Provided: Internal medicine, surgery, maternity, pediatrics, intensive care unit, pharmacy, laboratory and emergency services.

Syndicate of Physicians

Dr. El Hassan, Janah

Contact: Dr. Fayek Younes

Address: Four Seasons Bldg., first floor

P.O.Box: 11-640 Hazmieh, Lebanon

Tel: (961) 5-453051;05-457528/9;05-959959

Fax: 01-451480

Syndicate of Private Hospitals

Address: Museum Place

UNITED STATES DEPARTMENT OF STATE

OSAC

BUREAU OF DIPLOMATIC SECURITY

P.O.Box: 16-5662 Beirut, Lebanon

Tel: (961) 1-615468;01-425975;01-616772

Country-specific Vaccination and Health Guidance

For additional information on vaccines and health guidance, please visit the CDC at:
http://wwwnc.cdc.gov/travel/destinations/traveler/none/lebanon?s_cid=ncezid-dgmq-travel-do
uble-001.

OSAC Country Council Information

The Overseas Security Advisory Council (OSAC) serves as an information channel between
U.S. organizations operating in Lebanon and Embassy security officers. The Council Steering
Committee meets on a quarterly basis with full Council meetings taking place annually.
Representatives of American organizations operating in Lebanon are encouraged to contact
the Regional Security Office, 04/542600, ext. 4205. For Lebanon-specific information, go
online at http://beirut.osac.gov/ or http://www.osac.gov for general information. To reach
OSAC's Near East team, please email OSACNEA@state.gov.

U.S. Embassy Location and Contact Information

UNITED STATES DEPARTMENT OF STATE

OSAC

BUREAU OF DIPLOMATIC SECURITY

Embassy Address and Hours of Operation

The Embassy is located in Awkar, off the Dbayeh highway, facing the Awkar Municipal Building.

U.S. Embassy in Beirut, Lebanon

Address: Awkar facing the Municipality

P.O. Box 70-840 Antelias

Embassy Contact Numbers

Regional Security Officer:04/542600, ext. 4205

Medical Unit: 04/542600, ext. 4302

Consular Affairs: 04/542600, ext. 4380

Security Operations Center (24/7): 04/542600, ext. 4555

Website: http://lebanon.usembassy.gov/

Tips on How to Avoid Becoming a Victim

Situational Awareness Best Practices

Visitors are reminded to be watchful of their surroundings at all times, paying close attention to activities in their immediate area. Americans should exercise the same common sense precautions used in travel to any unfamiliar environment. Visitors are encouraged not to wear expensive jewelry, display large amounts of money, or dress in a manner that will draw attention. Avoid time/place predictability; seek to avoid repeated presence at the same venues and times, or at a minimum, use different routes to get there. Any unusual activity or inquiries should be reported to local security officials or to the Embassy's Regional Security Office at 04/542600, ext. 4205.

If considering renting an apartment, contemplate only those buildings offering controlled access and providing well-illuminated parking and walkway areas.

EXHIBIT '10':
Lebanon 2016 Country Summary - Human Rights Watch

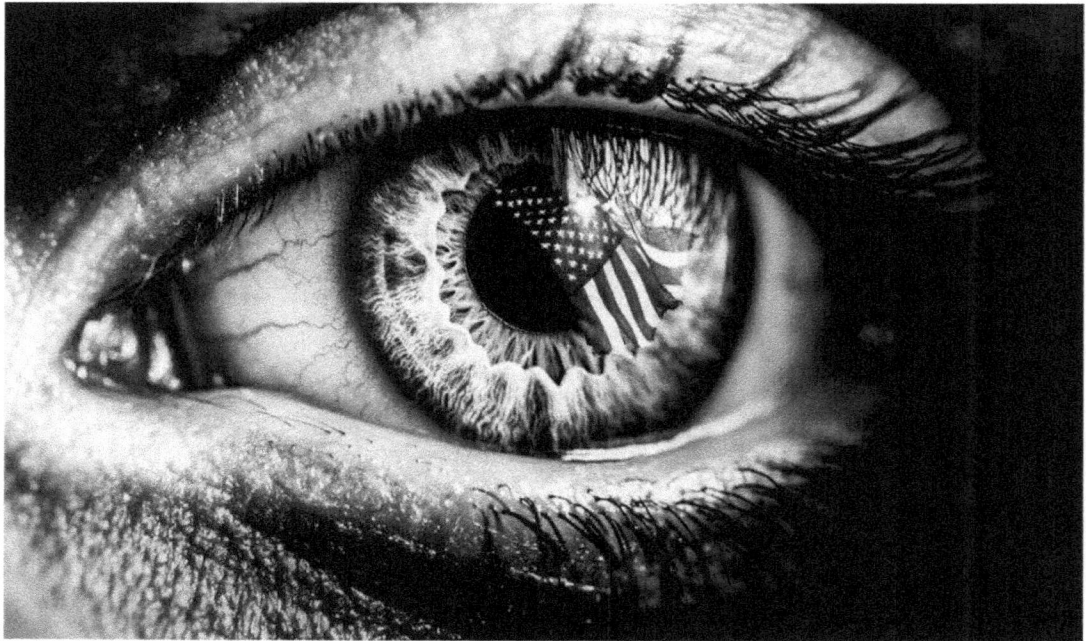

political institutions were paralyzed as the country remained without a president, and parliamentary elections—initially planned for June 2013 and then November 2014—were postponed again until 2017. The government's failure to provide basic services, including garbage removal, led to a wave of protests starting in August. In some instances, security forces used excessive force to quell these protests.

New entry regulations in January 2015 seriously restricted Syrian refugees from accessing Lebanese territory, while stringent residency renewal regulations rendered many Syrian refugees without legal status in Lebanon. With limited international support, the government struggled to meet refugees' needs. Draft laws to stop torture and improve the treatment of migrant domestic workers stalled in parliament.

Lengthy Pretrial Detention, Ill-Treatment, and Torture

Amid increased security threats, the Lebanese Armed Forces and Internal Security Forces (ISF) arrested suspects in relation to attacks on civilians in Lebanon or involvement with armed groups in Syria. Some of these suspects have suffered from lengthy pretrial detention and told Human Rights Watch that security forces had beaten, severely whipped, and tortured them, including with sticks, cigarettes, batons, and rifle butts.

In the context of conducting security operations, forces also targeted Syrian refugee settlements, sometimes arbitrarily detaining all adult males and later ill-treating or torturing some of them.

In June 2015, leaked videos showed ISF members torturing inmates in Roumieh prison north of Beirut following a prison riot. The interior minister confirmed the authenticity of the videos. Media reports said that 12 ISF members were referred for investigation; no update was provided regarding the outcome of the investigations.

▮▮▮▮▮ has not yet established a national preventive mechanism to visit and monitor places of detention, as required under the Optional Protocol to the Convention against Torture, which it ratified in 2008. Legislation to create such a body has stalled in parliament for several years.

Refugees

By November 2015, approximately 1.1 million Syrian refugees in Lebanon were registered with the United Nations High Commissioner for Refugees (UNHCR). In 2015, Lebanon set new entry regulations for Syrians that effectively barred many asylum seekers fleeing Syria from entering Lebanon, save for those who qualified for entry under exceptional humanitarian criteria.

In April, the Ministry of Social Affairs requested that UNHCR deregister all refugees who entered Lebanon after January 5 as part of ongoing governmental efforts to decrease the number of Syrian refugees in the country. Since May, UNHCR suspended the registration of Syrians in compliance with the government's request. Lebanon is not a signatory to the 1951 UN Refugee Convention, and refugees lacking legal status therefore risk detention for illegal presence in the country. Approximately 70 percent of Syrian refugees in Lebanon reportedly fall below the poverty line and rely on aid to survive.

Human Rights Watch also documented a few isolated incidents of deportations of Syrians and Palestinians back to Syria, putting them at risk of arbitrary detention, torture, or other persecution. Two Syrian inmates disappeared following their transfer into the custody of General Security in October and in November 2014; their relatives fear they have been forcibly deported to Syria.

Approximately 45,000 Palestinians from Syria are living in Lebanon, joining the estimated 400,000 Palestinian refugees already in the country. In 2015, Palestinians from Syria were still banned from entering the country. As of July, UN Relief and Works Agency for Palestine Refugees in the Near East (UNRWA) suspended its cash assistance for housing to Palestinians from Syria due to a shortage of funds.

Freedom of Assembly and Expression

In August and September, police used excessive force in a number of instances to disperse protesters demonstrating against the government's failure to resolve a trash removal problem, as well as corruption. On August 22 and 23, Lebanese security personnel used rubber bullets, tear gas, water cannons, rifle butts, and batons to control protesters. Security forces also fired live ammunition in the air. On August 19 and 29, and September 1 and 16, police officers also beat and arrested protesters.

Lebanon's State Prosecutor Samir Hammoud tasked a military prosecutor, who under Lebanese law has jurisdiction over crimes involving the security forces, to investigate the violence. Detained protesters charged with violence have been referred to military trials.

While freedom of expression is generally respected in the country, defaming or criticizing the Lebanese president or army is considered a criminal offense that can carry a jail sentence.

In January, Lebanese authorities summoned Al Jazeera journalist Faisal Qassem over charges of insulting the army in Facebook posts and, given his failure to show up to two hearings, issued an warrant of search and inquiry against him.

In October, political activist Michael Douaihy was released after General Security arrested and held him for nine days, and ordered him to pay a fine of $200 over a Facebook post criticizing the agency. Douaihy was indicted under article 386 of the Lebanese penal code that criminalizes libel and defamation against the president, public officials, and private individuals. Also in October, journalist Mohammed Nazzal was sentenced for six months in abstenia and fined US$666 for a Facebook post criticizing the Lebanese judiciary.

Migrant Workers

Migrant domestic workers, primarily from Sri Lanka, Ethiopia, the Philippines, and Nepal are excluded from the labor law and subject to restrictive immigration rules based on the *kafala* system, visa sponsorship that ties workers to their employers and puts them at risk of exploitation and abuse.

The most common complaints documented by the embassies of labor-sending countries and civil society groups include non-payment or delayed payment of wages, forced confinement to the workplace, refusal to provide time off, and verbal and physical abuse. Migrant domestic workers suing their employers for abuse face legal obstacles and risk detention and deportation due to the restrictive visa system.

In December 2014, six Lebanese workers submitted a request to the Labor Ministry to form a union for domestic workers. With support of the International Labour Organization (ILO), the International Trade Union Federation (ITUC), and the Federation of Trade Unions of Workers and Employees in Lebanon (FENASOL), approximately 350 domestic workers of various nationalities gathered for the union's inaugural congress on January 25, 2015.

The Labor Ministry denounced the formation of a domestic workers union on the grounds that it was illegal, as domestic work was not covered by the labor law. According to union members, the application for the union had yet to be decided at time of writing.

Starting in May 2014, nearly a dozen female migrant workers, many longstanding residents of Lebanon, reported being denied residency renewal for themselves and their children. Some were told their children were not allowed to remain with them in Lebanon and were given a short period of time to leave the country.

In March 2015, after months of advocacy by Human Rights Watch and other international and local nongovernmental organizations, General Security reversed this decision and migrant workers and their children are once again being issued residency renewals.

Women's Rights

Despite women's active participation in all aspects of Lebanese society, discriminatory provisions remain in personal status laws, nationality laws, and the criminal code.

Judges have issued scores of temporary protection orders since the enactment of the 2014 Law on the Protection of Women and Family from Domestic Violence. The new law establishes important protection measures and related policing and court reforms but leaves women at risk, as it still fails to criminalize all forms of domestic violence, including marital rape. Some women continued to report that police were unwilling to investigate their complaints, and the fund to assist victims of domestic violence has not yet been set up. Women continue to face obstacles in pursuing criminal complaints of domestic violence, mostly due to lengthy delays.

Under the 15 various Lebanese personal status laws, which are determined by an individual's religious affiliation, women across religions continue to suffer discrimination, including unequal access to divorce, child custody, and property rights. Unlike Lebanese men, Lebanese women cannot pass on their nationality to foreign husbands and children and continue to be subject to discriminatory inheritance laws.

Sexual Orientation and Gender Identity

Lebanon's penal code punishes "any sexual intercourse contrary to the order of nature" with up to one year in prison. In recent years, authorities conducted raids to arrest persons allegedly involved in same-sex conduct, some of whom were subjected to torture.

Legacy of Past Conflicts and Wars

Lebanese authorities continue to take no meaningful steps towards acting on proposals to set up an independent national commission to investigate the fate of people forcibly disappeared during the country's 1975-1990 civil war and its aftermath.

In October 2012, Justice Minister Shakib Qortbawi put forward a draft decree to the cabinet to establish a national commission to investigate the fate of the "disappeared," but no further action was taken. In September 2014, the government finally provided the families of the disappeared with the files of the Official Commission of Inquiry that had been appointed in 2000 to investigate the fate of the kidnapped. These showed that the government had not conducted any serious investigation.

Key International Actors

Syria, Iran, and Saudi Arabia maintain a strong influence on Lebanese politics through local allies and proxies, and increasingly so as the conflict in neighboring Syria drags on.

Many countries, including the United States, United Kingdom, members of the European Union, Canada, and various Gulf countries, have given Lebanon extensive, albeit insufficient, support to help it cope with the Syrian refugee crisis and to bolster security amid spill-over violence.

The Lebanese Armed Forces and ISF also receive assistance from a range of international donors, including the US, EU, UK, France, and Saudi Arabia. Some of these actors have taken steps to improve the compliance of these forces with international human rights law, but more pressure by the international community remains necessary.

LEBANON 2015/2016

Security forces used excessive force to disperse some demonstrations and to quell a protest by prisoners. Women continued to be discriminated against in law and in practice. Migrant workers faced exploitation and abuse. The authorities took no steps to investigate the fate of thousands of people who disappeared or went missing during the civil war of 1975 to 1990. Palestinian refugees long-resident in Lebanon continued to suffer discrimination. Lebanon hosted over 1.2 million refugees from Syria but closed its border and enforced new entry requirements from January, and barred the entry of Palestinians fleeing from Syria. Courts handed down at least 28 death sentences; there were no executions.

Background

Political disagreements between the main political parties prevented the election of a successor to President Suleiman, who left office in May 2014. In June 2015, thousands of people took to the streets of the capital, Beirut, to protest against the government's failure to provide basic services amid an escalating waste-management crisis, accusing the authorities of corruption and a lack of accountability and transparency.

The armed conflict in Syria had huge repercussions for Lebanon. Cross-border firing and the participation of Hizbullah fighters in the conflict in support of the Syrian government threatened Lebanon's security. Some 1.2 million Syrians had claimed refugee status in Lebanon by the end of the year. In January, Lebanon ended its open-border policy, preventing refugees without entry visas from entering the country.

In August, fighting between rival factions at Ain el-Helweh, Lebanon's largest Palestinian refugee camp, caused three deaths. Security conditions in Tripoli remained fragile due to tensions related to the Syrian conflict. In Syria, the armed group Islamic State (IS) continued to hold Lebanese soldiers and members of security forces whom they abducted in 2014, while Jabhat al-Nusra freed the ones it held.

Excessive use of force

There were several incidents of excessive use of force, particularly by the Internal Security Forces (ISF). In August, ISF officers and army soldiers used excessive force against people demonstrating in Beirut as part of the "You Stink" protests against the lack of rubbish clearance and other public services. Officers fired live ammunition, rubber bullets, tear gas canisters and water cannon, reportedly injuring over 300 people. The Minister for the Interior said eight members of the ISF would face disciplinary action over the incident.

Torture and other ill-treatment

In June, five officers were charged with using violence against prisoners at Roumieh Prison after two videos were posted on social media showing ISF officers beating inmates.

Despite ratifying the Optional Protocol to the UN Convention against Torture in 2000, by the end of the year Lebanon had yet to establish a national monitoring body on torture, as the Optional Protocol requires.

Refugees and asylum-seekers

Lebanon hosted around 300,000 Palestinian refugees and 1.2 million Syrian refugees. Palestinian refugees, many of whom entered Lebanon decades ago, remained subject to discriminatory laws and regulations that deny them the right to inherit property or access free public education and prevent them from working in 20 professions. At least 3,000 Palestinians who did not hold official identity documents also faced restrictions in registering births, marriages and deaths.

In January the government overturned its open-border policy and began restricting entry for Syrian refugees. Lebanon also continued to bar the entry of Palestinians fleeing the Syrian conflict. In May, Lebanon instructed UNHCR, the UN refugee agency, to provisionally suspend all new registrations of Syrian refugees. Refugees from Syria who entered Lebanon before January faced problems in renewing residency permits. Those who could not afford to renew annual residency permits, which they required to remain in Lebanon legally, became irregular in status and liable to arrest, detention and deportation.

The international community failed to provide adequate support to help Lebanon cope with the Syrian refugee crisis. Humanitarian assistance remained underfunded and there were few resettlement places offered by third countries to the most vulnerable refugees.

Women's rights

Women continued to face discrimination in law and in practice, particularly in relation to family matters including divorce, child custody and inheritance. Lebanese women married to foreign nationals remain barred from passing on their nationality to their children. The same restriction did not apply to Lebanese men married to foreign nationals. The authorities failed to criminalize marital rape or gender-based violence outside the home.

Migrant workers' rights

Migrant workers were excluded from the protections provided under national labour laws, exposing them to exploitation and abuse by employers. Migrant domestic workers, predominantly women, were especially vulnerable as they were employed under the *kafala* sponsorship system that ties the worker to their employer. In January, the Minister for Labour refused to recognize the trade union formed by migrant workers.

International justice

Special Tribunal for Lebanon

The Netherlands-based Special Tribunal for Lebanon (STL) continued to try five men in their absence for alleged complicity in the killing of former Prime Minister Rafic Hariri and others in a car bombing in Beirut in 2005. In September, the STL acquitted Lebanese journalist Karma Khayat and her employer Al Jadeed TV of obstructing justice but convicted her of contempt of court for ignoring a court order to remove information related to confidential witnesses, sentencing her to a fine of €10,000.

Impunity

The fate of thousands of people who were abducted, forcibly disappeared or who went missing during and after the civil war of 1975-1990 remained undisclosed. The authorities failed to establish an independent national body to investigate the fate of those disappeared and missing.

Death penalty

Courts imposed at least 28 death sentences for murder and terrorism-related crimes, including some in cases where the defendants were tried in their absence. No executions have been carried out since 2004.

U.S. PASSPORTS & INTERNATIONAL TRAVEL

U.S. DEPARTMENT OF STATE · BUREAU OF CONSULAR AFFAIRS

SEARCH 🔍

🖨 Print   ✉ Email

Lebanon Travel Warning

LAST UPDATED: JULY 29, 2016

The Department of State warns U.S. citizens to avoid travel to Lebanon because of the threats of terrorism, armed clashes, kidnapping, and outbreaks of violence near Lebanon's borders with Syria and Israel. U.S. citizens living and working in Lebanon should understand that they accept the risks of remaining in the country and should carefully consider those risks. This supersedes the Travel Warning issued on December 11, 2015.

There is potential for death or injury in Lebanon because of terrorist bombings. Violent extremist groups operate in Lebanon, including Hizballah, ISIL (Da'esh), ANF, Hamas, and the Abdullah Azzam Brigades (AAB). The U.S. government has designated all of these groups as terrorist organizations. ISIL and ANF have claimed responsibility for suicide bombings in Lebanon, and these groups are active throughout Lebanon. U.S. citizens have been the targets of terrorist attacks in Lebanon in the past, and the threat of anti-Western terrorist activity remains, as does the risk of death or injury as a non-targeted bystander.

Sudden outbreaks of violence can occur at any time in Lebanon, and armed clashes have occurred along the Lebanese borders and in Beirut. On June 27, 2016, a series of blasts caused by suicide bombers in Qa'a, a town along Lebanon's northeastern border killed five people and injured many others. On the evening of June 12, 2016, an explosion occurred outside a commercial bank in the central Beirut area of Verdun, causing major damage to the building and injuring two people. On November 12, 2015, twin suicide bombings in a commercial and residential area of the Burj al-Barajneh neighborhood in Beirut's southern suburbs killed 43 people and wounded 239 others. ISIL claimed responsibility for the bombings. The Lebanese Armed Forces are routinely brought in to quell the violence in these situations.

The Lebanese government cannot guarantee the protection of U.S. citizens in the country against sudden outbreaks of violence. Protesters have blocked major roads to gain publicity for their causes, including the primary road between downtown Beirut and Rafiq Hariri International Airport. Access to the airport may be cut off if the security situation deteriorates. Family, neighborhood, or sectarian disputes can escalate quickly and can lead to gunfire or other violence with no warning. In Tripoli, the neighborhoods of Bab al-Tabbaneh and Jabal Mohsen remain tense. Armed clashes have resulted in deaths and injuries in these neighborhoods in the past, and there are potentially large numbers of weapons in the hands of non-governmental elements. Celebratory gunfire in Lebanon has resulted in accidental injuries and deaths. The ability of U.S. government personnel to reach travelers or provide emergency services can be severely limited.

Kidnapping, whether for ransom, political motives, or family disputes, is a problem in Lebanon. A U.S. citizen was kidnapped in a family dispute in January 2016. Suspects in kidnappings sometimes have ties to terrorist or criminal organizations. The U.S. government's ability to help U.S. citizens kidnapped or taken hostage is very limited. Although the U.S. government places the highest priority on the safe recovery of kidnapped U.S. citizens, it is U.S. policy not to make concessions to hostage takers. U.S. law also makes it illegal to provide material support to terrorist organizations.

Clashes between Lebanese authorities and criminal elements continue to occur in areas of the Bekaa Valley and border regions. The U.S. Embassy strongly urges U.S. citizens to avoid the Lebanese-Syrian border region. There have been episodic clashes between the Lebanese Army and Syrian-based extremists along the border with Syria since August 2014. On March 24, 2016, a roadside bomb targeting a Lebanese Armed Forces patrol killed a Lebanese soldier and wounded several others in Lebanon's restive northeast border town of Arsal. On November 5, 2015, a deadly blast ripped through Arsal, killing at least four people and wounding several others. The November attack, caused by a suicide bomber using a motorbike, targeted a meeting in the al-Sabil neighborhood of the Committee of Qalamoun Scholars. The next day, a Lebanese Armed Forces patrol in al-Sabil was targeted by a roadside explosive device.

U.S. citizens in Lebanon should monitor political and security developments in both Lebanon and Syria. There have been incidents of cross-border shelling and air strikes of Lebanese villages from Syria, resulting in deaths and injuries. There have been reports of armed groups from Syria kidnapping or attacking Lebanese citizens living in border areas.

There are border tensions to the south with Israel, and the U.S. Embassy urges U.S. citizens to avoid this border. In January 2015, hostilities between Israel and Hizballah flared in the Golan Heights and Shebaa Farms area, and the potential for wider conflict remains. South of the Litani River, Hizballah has stockpiled large amounts of munitions in anticipation of a future conflict with Israel. In the past, there have been sporadic rocket attacks from southern Lebanon into Israel in connection with the violence between Israel and Hamas in Gaza. These attacks, normally consisting of rockets fired at northern Israel, often provoke a prompt Israeli military response. The rocket attacks and responses can occur without warning. Landmines and unexploded ordnance pose significant dangers throughout southern Lebanon, particularly south of the Litani River, as well as in areas of the country where fighting was intense during the civil war. More than 40 civilians have been killed and more than 300 injured by unexploded ordnance since the 2006 Israel-Hizballah war. Travelers should watch for posted landmine warnings and strictly avoid all areas where landmines and unexploded ordnance may be present.

Hizballah maintains a strong presence in parts of south Beirut, the Bekaa Valley, and areas in southern Lebanon. Hizballah has been the target of attacks by other extremist groups for their support of the Asad regime in Syria.

Palestinian groups hostile to both the Lebanese government and the United States operate autonomously in formal and informal refugee camps in different areas of the country. Intra-communal violence within the camps has resulted in shootings and explosions. On April 12, 2016, a car bomb explosion killed a senior Palestinian official near the Ein al-Hilweh Palestinian refugee camp in the southern port city of Sidon. U.S. citizens should avoid travel to refugee camps.

The U.S. Department of State warns U.S. citizens of the risk of traveling on airlines that fly over Syria. Commercial aircraft are at risk when flying over regions in conflict. We strongly recommend that U.S. citizens considering air travel overseas evaluate the route that their proposed commercial flight may take and avoid any flights that pass through Syrian airspace. U.S. government personnel in Lebanon have been prohibited from taking flights that pass through Syrian airspace.

The Department of State considers the threat to U.S. government personnel in Beirut sufficiently serious to require them to live and work under strict security restrictions. The internal security policies of the U.S. Embassy may be adjusted at any time and without advance notice. These practices limit, and may prevent, access by U.S. Embassy officials to certain areas of the country, especially to parts of metropolitan Beirut, Tripoli, the Bekaa Valley, refugee camps, and southern Lebanon.

In the event that the security climate in Lebanon worsens, U.S. citizens will be responsible for arranging their own travel out of Lebanon. The Embassy does not offer protection services to U.S. citizens who feel unsafe. U.S. citizens with special medical or other needs should be aware of the risks of remaining given their condition, and should be prepared to seek treatment in Lebanon if they cannot arrange for travel out of the country.

U.S. government-facilitated evacuations, such as the evacuation that took place from Lebanon in 2006, occur only when no safe commercial alternatives exist, and they are not guaranteed even when commercial travel options are limited or non-existent. Evacuation assistance is provided on a cost-recovery basis, which means the traveler must reimburse the U.S. government for travel costs. U.S. citizens in Lebanon should ensure that they have valid U.S. passports, as lack of documentation could hinder U.S. citizens' ability to depart the country. U.S. Legal Permanent Residents should consult with the Department of Homeland Security before they depart the United States to ensure they have proper documentation to re-enter. Further information on the Department's role during emergencies is provided on the Bureau of Consular Affairs' website.

For more information:

- See the State Department's travel website for the Worldwide Caution, Travel Warnings, Travel Alerts, and Country Specific Information for Lebanon.
- Enroll in the Smart Traveler Enrollment Program (STEP) Please provide your own current contact information and that for your

emergency contact/next-of-kin.

- Contact the U.S. Embassy in Beirut. The U.S. Embassy is located in Awkar, near Antelias, Beirut, Lebanon. You can contact the Embassy by telephone at (961-4) 542-600 outside the country/ 04 542-600 inside the country. The emergency after-hours number is (961-4) 543-600 between 2:00 p.m. and 4:00 p.m., Monday, Wednesday, and Friday local time. The most recent Security Messages are posted on the U.S. Embassy Beirut website. U.S. citizens in Lebanon may also contact the consular section by email at BeirutACS@state.gov. U.S. citizens seeking routine services must make appointments in advance.
- Call 1-888-407-4747 toll-free in the United States and Canada or 1-202-501-4444 from other countries.
- Follow us on Twitter and Facebook.

Embassies & Consulates   **+**

Assistance for U.S. Citizens

U.S. Embassy Beirut
Jmeil Street, Awkar (facing the
Awkar Municipality Building)
Beirut, Lebanon

- 📞 Telephone
  +(961) 4-542600 - 543600

- 📞 Emergency After-Hours
  Telephone
  +(961) 4-543600

- 📠 Fax
  +(961) 4-544209

- ✉ Email
  BeirutACS@state.gov

- 🌐 U.S. Embassy Beirut

click to enlarge

Executive Summary

The constitution states there shall be absolute freedom of conscience and guarantees the free exercise of religious rites for all religious groups provided the public order is not disturbed. The constitution states there shall be a "just and equitable balance" in the apportionment of cabinet and high level civil service positions among the major religious groups, a situation reaffirmed by the Taef Agreement, which ended the country's civil war and mandated equal representation between Christians and Muslims in the parliament. Some minority Christian groups complained they were not granted proportionate representation in the cabinet, high level civil service positions, or the parliament. In October Da'esh (the Islamic State of Iraq and the Levant) killed seven Sunni religious figures in Arsal for cooperating with the government, and in November claimed responsibility for two suicide bombings in Beirut, targeted at "heretics." The bombings killed 43 and injured more than 200 people. The Shia militia Hizballah continued to exercise authority over large parts of the country, limiting access to the area under its control and harassing Sunnis they perceived to be a threat.

In June a special Islamic summit in Beirut publicly condemned violent and discriminatory practices by extremists and the use of coercion in religious matters, while reiterating the principle of pluralism in Muslim-Christian relations and intra-Muslim relations. Religious leaders of Muslim and Christian communities reported places of worship continued to operate in relative peace and security, and that relationships among individual members of different religious groups generally remained amicable.

The U.S. Ambassador and embassy officers met regularly with government officials to discuss the importance of ending sectarian violence and encouraging tolerance and mutual respect among religious communities. Embassy officers encouraged religious leaders and members of civil society to engage in dialogue and to take steps to counter violent extremism. Embassy public outreach programs emphasized tolerance for all religious faiths, such as an embassy-funded program by the Adyan Foundation which organized discussions and events about religious tolerance for students in 36 public and private high schools.

Section I. Religious Demography

The U.S. government estimates the population at 6.2 million (July 2015 estimate). The United Nations High Commissioner for Refugees (UNHCR) and other organizations estimate the total population includes approximately 4.5 million citizens and approximately 1.4 million refugees fleeing the conflicts in Syria and Iraq, as well as a Palestinian refugee population present in Lebanon for nearly fifty years. Although the government has not conducted an official census since 1932, Statistics Lebanon, an independent firm, estimates 56.3 percent of the citizen population is Muslim, 28 percent Sunni and 20.6 percent Shia ("Twelvers") plus smaller percentages of Alawites and Ismailis ("Sevener" Shia).

Statistics Lebanon estimates 35.5 percent of the population is Christian. The Maronite community, the largest Christian group, maintains its centuries-long affiliation with the Roman Catholic Church but has its own patriarch, liturgy, and ecclesiastical customs. The second-largest Christian group is Greek Orthodox. Other Christian groups include Greek Catholics, Armenian Orthodox (Gregorians), Armenian Catholics, Syriac Orthodox (Jacobites), Syriac Catholics, Assyrians (Nestorians), Chaldeans, Copts, evangelicals (including Baptists and Seventh-day Adventists), Latins (Roman Catholics), and members of The Church of Latter-day Saints (Mormons).

According to Statistics Lebanon, 5.2 percent of the population is Druze, who refer to themselves as *al-Muwahhideen*, or "believers in one God," and are concentrated in the rural, mountainous areas east and south of Beirut. There are small numbers of Jews, Bahais, Buddhists, and Hindus.

There are approximately 1.1 million registered refugees from Syria, of whom approximately 42,000 are Palestinian refugees. Refugees from Syria are largely Sunni, but include Shia and Christians as well. There are between 250,000 and 300,000 Palestinians from Gaza and the West Bank still living in the country as refugees from previous conflicts in the region. The Palestinian refugee population is largely Sunni.

Refugees and migrants also include largely Sunni Kurds; Sunnis, Shia, and Chaldeans from Iraq; as well as Coptic Christians from Egypt and Sudan. According to the secretary-general of the Syriac League, approximately 10,000 Iraqi Christians and 3,000 to 4,000 Coptic Christians reside in the country.

Section II. Status of Government Respect for Religious Freedom

Legal Framework

The constitution states there shall be "absolute freedom of conscience." It declares the state will respect all religious groups and denominations as well as the personal status and religious interests of persons of every religious group. The constitution guarantees free exercise of religious rites provided public order is not disturbed and declares the equality of rights and duties for all citizens without discrimination or preference.

By law, an individual is free to convert to a different religion if the change is approved by a local senior official of the religious group the person wishes to join. The law does not address the freedom to proselytize.

The penal code stipulates a maximum prison term of one year for anyone convicted of "blaspheming God publicly." It does not provide a definition of what this entails.

By law, religious groups may apply to the government for official recognition. A religious group seeking official recognition must submit a statement of its doctrine and moral principles to the cabinet, which evaluates whether the group's principles are in accord with the government's perception of popular values and the constitution. Alternatively, an unrecognized religious group may apply for recognition by applying to a recognized religious group. In doing so, the unrecognized group does not gain recognition as a separate group, but becomes an affiliate of the group through which it applies. This process has the same requirements as applying for recognition directly with the government.

There are 18 officially-recognized religious groups. These include four Muslim groups (Shia, Sunni, Alawites and Ismaili), 12 Christian groups (Maronites, Greek Orthodox, and 10 smaller groups), Druze, and Jews. Groups the government does not recognize include Bahais, Buddhists, Hindus, and several Protestant groups.

Official recognition of a religious group allows baptisms and marriages performed by the group to receive government sanction. Official recognition also conveys other benefits, such as tax-exempt status and the right to apply the religious group's codes to personal status matters. The government permits recognized religious groups to administer their own family and personal status laws in areas such as marriage, divorce, child custody, and inheritance. Shia, Sunni, recognized

Christian, and Druze groups have state-appointed, government-subsidized clerical courts to administer family and personal status law.

Religious groups perform all marriages; there are no formalized procedures for civil marriage. The government recognizes civil marriage ceremonies performed outside the country, however, irrespective of the religious affiliation of each partner in the marriage.

Nonrecognized religious groups may own property and may assemble for worship and perform their religious rites freely. They may not perform legally-recognized marriage or divorce proceedings, however, and they have no standing to determine inheritance issues. Members of these groups do not qualify for certain government positions.

The law allows censorship of religious publications under a number of conditions, including if the material is deemed by the government to incite sectarian discord or to be a threat to national security.

According to the constitution, religious communities may have their own schools provided they follow the general rules issued for public schools, which stipulate schools should not incite sectarian discord or be deemed a threat to national security.

The constitution states "sectarian groups" shall be represented in a "just and equitable balance" in the cabinet and high level civil service positions, which includes the ministry ranks of secretary general and director general. It also states these posts shall be distributed proportionately among the recognized religious groups. The parliament is elected on the basis of "equality between Christians and Muslims." The 1943 National Pact, which the constitution upholds, although it is not an official component of the constitution and is not a formally binding agreement, states the president shall be Maronite Christian, the speaker of parliament shall be Shia Muslim, and the prime minister shall be Sunni Muslim. This distribution of political power operates at both the national and local levels of government.

The Taef Agreement, which ended the country's 15-year civil war in 1989, also mandates equal Muslim and Christian representation in parliament but reduces the power of the Maronite Christian presidency. In addition, the agreement endorses the constitutional provision of appointing most senior government officials according to religious affiliation. The Taef Agreement also mandates a cabinet with seats allocated equally between Muslims and Christians. The Taef Agreement's stipulations on equality of representation between members of different confessions do not apply to citizens who do not list a religious affiliation on their national registration.

By law, each Christian group' bishops' synods elect their patriarchs; the Sunni and Shia electoral bodies elect their respective senior clerical posts; and the Druze community elects its sheikh al-aql. The government council of ministers must endorse the nomination of Sunni and Shia muftis, as well as the Druze sheikh al-aql, and pay their salaries. The government also appoints and pays the salaries of Muslim and Druze clerical judges. The government does not endorse Christian patriarchs and does not pay the salaries of clergy and officials of Christian groups, including the Maronites, Greek Orthodox, and Roman Catholics.

Citizens have the right to remove the customary notation of their religion from their identity cards and official registry documents or change how it is listed. The government does not require religious affiliation on passports.

The government issues religious workers a one-month visa; in order to stay longer a worker must complete a residency application during the month. A religious worker also must sign a "commitment of responsibility" form before receiving a visa, which subjects the worker to legal prosecution and immediate deportation for any activity involving religious or other criticism directed against the state or any other country except Israel. If the government finds an individual engaging in religious activity while on a tourist visa, the government may determine a violation of the visa status has occurred and deport the individual.

Government Practices

The rarely-invoked blasphemy provision of the penal code was not applied during the year, although the media reported Ziad Aswad, Member of Parliament (MP) of the Free Patriotic Movement, filed a lawsuit against You Stink activist Assad Thebian for "defamation and contempt of religion." Thebian reportedly had made comments about Christianity on Facebook several years ago. As of the end of the year, no action had been taken with regard to the lawsuit.

The government continued to require Protestant evangelical churches to register with the Evangelical Synod, a self-governing advisory group overseeing religious matters for Protestant congregations and representing those churches with the government.

Some members of unregistered religious groups said they continued to choose to list themselves as belonging to recognized religious groups in government records to ensure their marriage and other personal status documents remained legally valid.

The government continued to refuse to give approval to the request from the Jewish community, repeated over several years, to change its official name from the Israeli Communal Council to the Jewish Community Council.

Continuing its practice of rarely invoking the censorship provision of the law, the government permitted the publication of religious materials of every religious group in different languages.

Minority Christian groups stated the government continued to make little progress towards the goal called for in the Taef Agreement to eliminate political sectarianism in favor of "expertise and competence." Members of these groups stated the government discriminated against them by continuing not to appoint someone from one of their groups to a ministerial position. While some of their members had served in high level civil service positions, such as director general, they said Maronite and Greek Orthodox individuals filled most high level positions. Minority Christian leaders stated their allocation of seats in the parliament remained disproportionately low at only one seat out of the 64 seats allocated to all Christian groups, because their estimated membership of 50,000 individuals represented a higher percentage of the overall Christian population.

Despite registering a civil marriage for the first time in 2013, the practice was unofficially halted by the Ministry of Interior following the formation of a new cabinet. At year's end, at least 30 cases were pending registration with the ministry.

Abuses by Foreign Forces and Non-State Actors

In November Da'esh claimed responsibility for two suicide bombings, killing 43 and injuring more than 200 in the Burj al-Barajeneh neighborhood (Dahiyeh suburbs) of Beirut. Da'esh claimed the attack specifically targeted "heretics" in a predominantly Shiite area and vowed to continue such attacks.

In October Da'esh killed seven Sunni religious figures in Arsal for what it said was their cooperation with the government over hostage negotiations related to a 2014 attack in Arsal by Da'esh and al-Nusra leading to the capture of 29 government soldiers, four of whom were later killed. On December 1, the government and al-Nusra engaged in a prisoner exchange involving the release of 16 Lebanese security officers by al-Nusra in exchange for the government's release of 13 al-Nusra members. The remaining prisoners had not been released as of the end of the year.

Hizballah, a Shia terrorist militia, continued to exercise authority over large areas of territory. There were credible reports of Hizballah and other Shia militias continuing to control access to neighborhoods under their authority and continuing to harass Sunnis they perceived to be a threat.

Section III. Status of Societal Respect for Religious Freedom

Following terrorist attacks by Da'esh and al-Nusra, leaders of Sunni, Shia, and many Christian groups condemned extremism and violence perpetrated in the name of religion. On June 3, a special Islamic summit held in Beirut at the headquarters of Dar el-Fatwa, Sunni Islam's main body, issued a press release condemning violent and discriminatory practices by extremists, condemning coercion in religious matters, calling for respect of private and public rights, and reiterating the principle of pluralism in Muslim-Christian relations and intra-Muslim relations.

In February the media reported that societal criticism of remarks by Future Movement MP Khaled Daher suggesting Christian religious symbols should be taken down from outside churches had led the MP to make an apology and state his remarks had been taken out of context. Daher had criticized the removal of black flags bearing the slogan "there is no God but God" from a main square in Tripoli, saying the removal of the flags was an affront to the Sunni community. He was reported as saying a Christ the King statue and posters of Christian saints should be removed instead. The media reported the flags had been taken down because of their resemblance to Da'esh banners.

Religious leaders reported places of worship of every religious group continued to operate in relative peace and security, and that relationships among individual members of different religious groups generally remained amicable. Christian and

Muslim religious leaders from the major denominations stated they continued to meet regularly to discuss issues of common concern and to try to quell conflict between religious groups at conferences hosted by the National Committee for Muslim-Christian Dialogue and similar events.

On June 15, the nongovernmental organization (NGO) MARCH embarked on a conflict resolution project in Tripoli in hopes of uniting youth from different religious communities around art and culture, and launched a comedy play titled "Love and War on the Rooftops—A Tripolitan Tale." A part of the project was aimed at uniting youth from different religious communities around art and culture. The actors included 16 young adults of different faiths from the villages of Jabal Mohsen and Bab al-Tabbaneh.

A television show broadcast on May 20 showed footage of a Syrian man destroying statues of naked or half naked women located on the coastal road of Amchit village north of Beirut. Upon his arrest, he stated he had destroyed the statues because they were against Islamic doctrine. There was no further information on the disposition of his case as of year's end.

Section IV. U.S. Government Policy

The U.S. Ambassador and embassy officers continued to meet regularly with government officials to discuss the importance of ending sectarian violence and encouraging tolerance, dialogue, and mutual respect among religious groups.

Embassy officers encouraged religious leaders and members of civil society to engage in dialogue and to take steps to counter violent extremism. The Ambassador met with the leadership of the Sunni, Shia, Druze, and many Christian communities to promote a similar message. The Ambassador and embassy officers also continued to work with local religious and community leaders to support their efforts to reduce sectarian tensions spilling over from the violence in Syria.

Embassy public outreach programs emphasized tolerance for all religious faiths. For example, the embassy renewed funding for the Adyan Foundation's (a local NGO) Alwan program. Alwan operated in 36 public and private high schools throughout the country to provide a non-formal education program on religious pluralism, citizenship, and coexistence. The embassy also sponsored the visit of a Lebanese scholar to the United States to study religious pluralism.

EXECUTIVE SUMMARY

█████ is a parliamentary republic based on the 1943 National Pact, which apportions governmental authority among a Maronite Christian president, a Shia speaker of the Chamber of Deputies (parliament), and a Sunni prime minister. Observers considered the 2009 parliamentary elections peaceful, free, and fair. The parliament since twice-postponed parliamentary elections, initially scheduled for 2013. The elections were rescheduled for June 2017. Civilian authorities maintained control over the armed forces and other security forces, although the designated terrorist group Hizballah, Palestinian security and militia forces, and other extremist elements operated outside the direction or control of government officials.

Following the influx of refugees since the start of the crisis in Syria in 2011, Lebanon experienced increased spillover violence, including several rounds of fighting initiated by the extremist groups the Da'esh and al-Nusra Front (Nusra).

The most significant human rights abuses during the year were torture and abuse by security forces, harsh prison and detention center conditions, and limitations on freedom of movement for Palestinian and Syrian refugees.

Other human rights abuses included lengthy pretrial detention; a judiciary subject to political pressure and long delays in trials; violation of citizens' privacy rights; some restrictions on freedoms of speech and press, including intimidation of journalists; some restrictions on freedom of assembly; reports of harassment of Syrian political activists and other refugees; restrictions on citizens' ability to change their government; official corruption and lack of transparency; widespread violence against women; societal, legal, and economic discrimination against women; societal and legal discrimination against lesbian, gay, bisexual, transgender and intersex (LGBTI) individuals; trafficking in persons; discrimination against persons with disabilities; systematic discrimination against Palestinian refugees and minority groups; killings related to societal violence; restricted labor rights for and abuse of migrant domestic workers; and child labor.

Although the legal structure provides for prosecution and punishment, government officials enjoyed a measure of impunity for human rights abuses.

Despite the presence of Lebanese and UN security forces, Hizballah retained significant influence over parts of the country, and the government made no tangible progress toward disbanding and disarming armed militia groups, including Hizballah. Palestinian refugee camps continued to act as self-governed entities and maintained security and militia forces not under the direction of government officials. Da'esh and Nusra maintained a significant military presence along Lebanon's eastern border, particularly near the city of Arsal, and conducted suicide bombing attacks.

Section 1. Respect for the Integrity of the Person, Including Freedom from:

a. Arbitrary or Unlawful Deprivation of Life

There were no reports that the government or its agents committed arbitrary or unlawful killings during the year. Islamist extremist groups, however, committed numerous unlawful killings.

The country was increasingly affected by the Syrian crisis, which further polarized its politics, paralyzed many state institutions, generated a massive humanitarian refugee crisis, depressed the economy, inflamed sectarian tensions, and degraded national security. The continued spillover of violence led to the unlawful deprivation of life throughout the country, particularly in Tripoli, Arsal, and the southern suburbs of Beirut, by nonstate actors, including gangs and terrorist organizations.

On January 10, two suicide bombers blew themselves up in a crowded cafe in the Alawite-dominated area of Jabal Mohsen, killing nine persons and injuring more than 30. Nusra claimed responsibility for the attack.

The recurring conflict in the northern city of Tripoli between the generally pro-Syrian regime Alawite residents of Jabal Mohsen and the nearby generally pro-Syrian opposition Sunni district of Bab al-Tabbaneh continued. On March 3, an unknown assailant shot and killed Bader Eid, brother of Alawite and pro-Asad Ali Eid, head of the Arab Democratic Party. Press reported that "The Gathering of Kuweikhat Youth," an unknown group from Akkar, claimed responsibility on social media; however, the accuracy of this report was unknown.

In August 2014 clashes erupted between army personnel and Islamist militants aligned with Da'esh and Nusra in Arsal. Nineteen Lebanese Armed Forces (LAF) members and 40 to 45 Syrians and Lebanese died; 90 to 100 individuals were injured. Islamist militants took 29 LAF and Internal Security Forces (ISF) members hostage, executed four, released six, and kept the remainder prisoner. On December 1, 2015, 16 Lebanese servicemen held by Nusra were released in a prisoner exchange with the LAF; nine servicemen continued to be held captive by Da'esh.

On November 5, Da'esh killed seven Sunni religious figures in Arsal, reportedly due to their cooperation in prisoner hostage negotiations with the government and Nusra.

On November 12, Da'esh claimed responsibility for two suicide bombings in the Burj al-Barajeneh neighborhood (Dahiyeh suburbs) of Beirut that killed 43 and injured more than 200 persons. Da'esh claimed the attack was specifically targeting "heretics" in a predominantly Shiite area and vowed to continue attacks.

In 2013 the Special Tribunal for Lebanon (STL), which operated based upon an agreement between the United Nations and the government, indicted Hassan Habib Merhi, a Hizballah member, as a fifth suspect in the 2005 killing of former prime minister Rafik Hariri and 22 other individuals. In 2011 the STL indicted four individuals, Mustafa Amine Badreddine, Hussein Hassan Oneissi, Salim Jamil Ayyash, and Assad Hassan Sabra, all of whom were Hizballah operatives suspected of collaborating in the 2005 killings. Due to the incidents' similar nature and gravity, the STL also established jurisdiction over the 2005 killing of former Communist Party leader George Hawi and attacks on former ministers Elias Murr and Marwan Hamadeh. Government authorities, however, notified the STL that they were unable to detain or serve the accused with the indictments in that case. In January 2014 the STL opened its first trial in the case of Ayyash and other defendants. During the year the government discreetly paid its dues to the STL, despite rumors that the government would forego paying to avoid provoking Hizballah.

b. Disappearance

There were no confirmed reports of politically motivated disappearances during the year.

Syrians who fled to Lebanon from civil war, including political activists and other refugees, risked being targeted, harassed, and arrested by Lebanese security services, as well as by others. Syrian opposition activists asserted that Syrian agents in Lebanon targeted them. They claimed they had to operate clandestinely for their protection. Additionally, retaliatory sectarian kidnappings occurred as a result of Da'esh's and Nusra's actions in Arsal.

c. Torture and Other Cruel, Inhuman, or Degrading Treatment or Punishment

The law does not specifically prohibit all forms of torture or cruel, inhuman, or degrading treatment or punishment, and there were reports security officials employed such practices. The penal code prohibits using acts of violence to obtain a confession or information about a crime, but the judiciary rarely investigated or prosecuted allegations of such acts. According to domestic and international human rights groups, security forces abused detainees and used torture to obtain confessions or encourage suspects to implicate other individuals.

Human rights organizations reported that torture occurred in certain police stations, in the Ministry of Defense's detention facilities, and in the Information Branch of the ISF. The government denied the use of torture, although authorities acknowledged violent abuse sometimes occurred during preliminary investigations at police stations or military installations, where suspects were interrogated without an attorney. Such abuse reportedly occurred in multiple units despite national laws prohibiting judges from accepting confessions extracted under duress.

Reports the ISF threatened, mistreated, and tortured drug users, persons involved in prostitution, and LGBTI persons in their custody were common. The most common forms of abuse reported were blows from fists, boots, or implements, such as sticks, canes, and rulers. The ISF responded to similar claims in prior years and stated the reports defamed the organization and called for verification of unproven allegations, although evidence in some cases, including video evidence, proved the use of torture in some facilities.

Former prisoners, detainees, and reputable local human rights groups reported that methods of torture and abuse included continuous blindfolding, hanging detainees by wrists tied behind their backs, violent beatings, blows to the soles of the feet, electric shocks, sexual abuse, psychological abuse, immersion in cold water, extended periods of sleep deprivation, being forced to stand for extended periods, threats of violence against relatives, and deprivation of clothing, food, and toilet facilities. Allegations that the ISF specifically targeted the LGBTI community for abuse were common.

On June 20, a video of ISF officers beating inmates at the country's largest prison, Roumieh Prison, was posted to YouTube. The officers beat the men severely with a rod. One guard groped a prisoner before hitting him and another prisoner. Another video showed a guard striking another prisoner, then ordering the prisoner to kiss his feet before kicking him in the face with his boot. In response to the public outcry, Interior Minister Nouhad Mashnouq condemned the torture of the inmates, asserting that he would take action, and Justice Minister Ashraf Rifi pledged to pursue the investigation until the last perpetrator was in custody. As of December 1, the three guards seen in the prison video were in custody and on trial for beating the prisoners, while a fourth, the cameraman, was exonerated and released.

Prison and Detention Center Conditions

Prison and detention center conditions were harsh, and prisoners often lacked access to basic sanitation. In some prisons, such as the central prison in Roumieh, conditions were life threatening. Facilities were not adequately equipped for persons with disabilities.

Physical Conditions: As of December 8, there were 6,502 prisoners and detainees, including pretrial detainees and remanded prisoners, in facilities built to hold 3,500 inmates. Roumieh Prison, with a designed capacity of 1,500, held approximately 3,210 persons. Authorities often held pretrial detainees together with convicted prisoners. Men and women were held separately in similar conditions, and ISF statistics indicated that 132 minors and 283 women were incarcerated.

Sanitary conditions in overcrowded prisons were poor, and they worsened in Roumieh following a destructive riot in 2011. According to a government official, most prisons lacked adequate sanitation, ventilation, and lighting, and temperatures were not regulated consistently. Prisoners lacked consistent access to potable water (as do many Lebanese citizens). Roumieh prisoners often slept 10 in a room originally built to accommodate two prisoners. Basic medical care at Roumieh improved with better equipment and training, but staffing continued to be inadequate, and working conditions were poor. Additionally, the medical facilities were extremely overcrowded. According to ISF statistics, 10 prisoners died from natural causes during the year. Some nongovernmental organizations (NGOs) complained of authorities' negligence and failure to provide appropriate medical care to prisoners, which may have contributed to some of the deaths. The ISF reported that none died of police abuse and that there were no cases of rape in prisons during the year.

There were reports of female prisoners exchanging sex in return for "favors," such as cigarettes, food, more comfortable conditions in their cells, or a more lenient police report.

Administration: Recordkeeping was not adequate. In many prisons inmates who completed their sentences were not released due to poor recordkeeping. Some juveniles benefitted from alternative sentencing. Although there is a legal means to impose a sentence of probation or supervised release for adults in lieu of incarceration, it was not applied. A person sentenced to imprisonment for more than six months may obtain a sentence reduction upon demonstrating that he has had good behavior, that he does not pose a threat to himself or others, and that he has met certain conditions depending on the category of crime and the release order. The Commission on the Reduction of Sentences considered sentence reduction requests. A chamber of the Court of Appeals, which made the final decision on whether to reduce a sentence, reviewed the commission's recommendations.

There were no prison ombudsmen. Authorities did not implement a 2005 law establishing an ombudsman to serve on behalf of citizens. The ISF, however, posted signs in detention facilities stating detainees' rights and had an inspection unit. The Minister of Interior assigned a general-rank official as the commander of the inspection unit and a colonel-rank official as the commander of the medical and human rights unit. The units were instructed to investigate every complaint. After completing an investigation, authorities transferred the case to the inspector general for action in the case of a disciplinary act or to a military investigative judge for additional investigation. If investigators found physical abuse, the military investigator assigned a medical team to confirm the abuse and the judge ruled at the conclusion of the review. There were no statistics available at year's end regarding the number of complaints, investigations, and disciplinary or judicial actions taken.

Families of prisoners normally contacted the Ministry of Interior to report complaints, although prison directors could also initiate investigations. According to a government official, prison directors often protected officers under investigation.

The ISF's Committee to Monitor against the Use of Torture and Other Inhuman Practices in Prisons and Detention Centers conducted a minimum of one or two prison visits per week. The parliamentary human rights committee was responsible for monitoring the Ministry of Defense detention center.

Independent Monitoring: The government permitted independent monitoring of prison and detention conditions by local and international human rights groups and the International Committee of the Red Cross (ICRC), and such monitoring took place. During 2014 the ICRC visited 6,500 prisoners in 29 prisons and detention centers.

Nongovernmental entities, such as Hizballah and Palestinian militias, also operated unofficial detention facilities, but no information about these facilities was available.

Improvements: Authorities made some minor improvements in block B of Roumieh Prison, including painting, installing a new bathroom and sinks, as well as televisions and fans. The kitchen of Roumieh Prison received new cooking equipment, and the number of public telephones with phone cards was increased to 10. The ISF reported that Tripoli Prison was equipped with a ventilation system and energy solar system during the year. A public library, gym, and a medical center were set up inside the Zahle Prison. The quality and quantity of the food in Jbeil Prison improved during the year. A public telephone with a phone card was installed in Jbeil and Marjeyoun prisons. The electricity network in the women's Baabda Prison was repaired and cameras were installed.

d. Arbitrary Arrest or Detention

The law requires judicial warrants before arrests except in cases of active pursuit. Nonetheless, the government arbitrarily arrested and detained persons.

Role of the Police and Security Apparatus

The ISF, under the Ministry of Interior is responsible for law enforcement. The General Directorate for State Security, reporting to the prime minister, and the Directorate of General Security (DGS), under the Ministry of Interior, is responsible for border control. The LAF, under the Ministry of Defense, is responsible for external security but also may arrest and detain suspects on national security grounds. All of these organizations collected information on groups deemed possible threats to state security. Each security apparatus has its own internal mechanisms to investigate cases of abuse and misconduct. A 2012 ISF code of conduct defines the obligations of ISF members and the legal and ethical standards by which they must abide in performing their duties. Various security forces underwent training on the code. Civilian authorities maintained effective control over security forces. Government security force officials, however, reportedly enjoyed a measure of implicit impunity due to the lack of publicly available information on the outcome of prosecutions. The government lacked mechanisms to investigate and punish abuse and corruption. There are internal complaint mechanisms within the security forces.

In accordance with UN Security Resolutions 425 and 426, the UN Interim Force in Lebanon (UNIFIL) was established in 1978 to confirm the Israeli withdrawal from southern Lebanon, restore peace and security, and assist the government in restoring its authority over its territory. UN Security Resolution 1701 stated UNIFIL was to monitor (per UN resolutions) cessation of hostilities between Israel and Hizballah after their 2006 war, accompany the LAF in deploying in southern Lebanon, assist in providing humanitarian access to civilians and safe return of displaced, and assist the government in securing its borders.

Arrest Procedures and Treatment of Detainees

The law generally requires a warrant for arrest and provides the right to a medical examination and referral to a prosecutor within 48 hours of arrest. If authorities hold a detainee longer than 48 hours without formal charges, the arrest is considered arbitrary, and the detainee must be released or a formal extension requested. The code of criminal procedures provides that a person may be held in police custody for investigation for 48 hours, unless the investigation requires additional time, in which case the period of custody may be renewed for another 48 hours.

The code of criminal procedures also states that from the moment of arrest a suspect or the subject of a complaint has the right to contact a member of his family, his employer, an advocate of his choosing, an acquaintance, or an interpreter, and undergo a medical examination on the approval of the general prosecutor. It does not mention, however, whether a lawyer may attend preliminary questioning with the judicial police. In practical terms, the lawyer may not attend the preliminary questioning with judicial police. Under the framework of the law, it is possible for a suspect to be held at a police station for hours before being granted the right to contact an attorney. If the suspect lacks the resources to obtain legal counsel, authorities must provide free legal aid. The law does not, however, require the judicial police to inform an individual who lacks legal counsel that one may be assigned through the Bar Association, whether in Beirut or Tripoli.

The law does not require authorities to inform individuals they have the right to remain silent. Many provisions of the law simply state that if the individual being questioned refuses to make a statement or remains silent, this should be recorded and that the detainee may not be "coerced to speak or to undergo questioning, on pain of nullity of their statements."

The law states the period of detention for a misdemeanor may not exceed two months. This period may be extended by a maximum of two additional months. The initial period of custody may not exceed six months for a felony, but the detention may be renewed. Excluded from this protection are suspects accused of homicide or with a previous criminal conviction, drug crimes, endangerment of state security, violent crimes, and crimes involving terrorism.

Officials responsible for prolonged arrest may be prosecuted on charges of depriving personal freedom, but authorities rarely filed charges. The law requires authorities to inform detainees of the charges filed against them. A suspect caught in the act of committing a crime must be referred to an examining judge, who decides whether to issue an indictment or order the release of the suspect. By law bail is available in all cases regardless of the charges, although the amounts required may be prohibitively high.

Authorities failed to observe many provisions of the law, and government security forces, as well as extralegal armed groups such as Hizballah, continued the practice of extrajudicial arrest and detention, including incommunicado detention. Additionally, the law permits military intelligence personnel to make arrests without warrants in cases involving military personnel or involving civilians suspected of espionage, treason, or weapons possession.

Arbitrary Arrest: According to local NGOs, there were no clear cases of arbitrary detention of citizens, but cases from previous years continued. Civil society groups reported authorities frequently detained foreign nationals arbitrarily.

Pretrial Detention: According to ISF statistics, 3,853 of the 6,502 persons in prison were in pretrial detention as of December 8. The Office of the UN High Commissioner for Human Rights expressed concern about arbitrary pretrial detention without access to legal representation and refused to support construction of prisons until the serious problem of arbitrary pretrial detention was resolved.

According to a study by the Lebanese Center for Human Rights, detainees spent one year on average in pretrial detention prior to sentencing. Individuals accused of murder spent on average 3.5 years in pretrial detention. Many Salafist prisoners remained in prolonged pretrial detention, including detainees from the Nahr el-Bared fighting in 2007.

State security forces and autonomous Palestinian security factions subjected Palestinian refugees to arbitrary arrest and detention.

e. Denial of Fair Public Trial

Although the constitution provides for an independent judiciary, the judiciary was subjected to political pressure, particularly in the appointment of key prosecutors and investigating magistrates. Influential politicians and intelligence officers intervened at times and used their influence and connections to protect supporters from prosecution. Persons involved in routine civil and criminal proceedings sometimes solicited the assistance of prominent individuals to influence the outcome of their cases.

Trial Procedures

Defendants are presumed innocent until proven guilty. Trials are generally public, but judges have the discretion to order a closed court session. There is no trial by jury. Defendants have the right to be present at trial, to consult with an attorney in a timely manner, and to question witnesses against them. Defendants may present witnesses and evidence, and their attorneys have access to government-held evidence relevant to their cases. Defendants have the right not to be compelled to testify or confess guilt; they have the right of appeal.

The Military Court has jurisdiction over cases involving the military as well as those involving civilians accused of espionage, treason, weapons possession, and draft evasion. Civilians may be tried on security charges, and military personnel may be tried on civil charges. The Military Court has a permanent tribunal and a cassation tribunal. The latter hears appeals from the former. A civilian judge chairs the higher court. Defendants on trial under the military tribunal have the same procedural rights as defendants in ordinary courts. Human rights groups expressed concerns about the trial of civilians in military courts, the extent to which they were afforded full due process, and the lack of review of verdicts by ordinary courts.

Because of an agreement struck between the Lebanese government and late Palestinian leader Yasser Arafat, Lebanese security forces do not enter Palestinian camps in Lebanon; they remain outside the entrance and check vehicles and identification. As a result the camps, particularly Ain el-Helweh, had the reputation of being lawless enclaves on Lebanese territory, and Lebanese authorities stated foreign and local jihadis found refuge among them.

The Palestinian factions that theoretically provided security in the camps often fought each other for control, and these groups generally also controlled the justice systems in the camps. Governance varied greatly, with some camps under the control of joint Palestinian security forces, while others were heavily influenced by local militia strongmen. Palestinian groups in refugee camps operated an autonomous and arbitrary system of justice outside the control of the state. For example, local popular committees in the camps attempted to resolve disputes through informal mediation methods but occasionally transferred those accused of more serious offenses (murder, terrorism, etc.) to state authorities for trial. Several Palestinian factions formed a joint security force to help maintain stability and security within the Ain el-Helweh camp, but this force was increasingly challenged for control of the camp by upstart Islamist groups.

Political Prisoners and Detainees

There were no reports of political prisoners or detainees.

Civil Judicial Procedures and Remedies

There is an independent judiciary in civil matters, but civil lawsuits seeking damages for government human rights violations were seldom submitted to it. During the year there were no examples of a civil court awarding a person compensation for such violations.

f. Arbitrary Interference with Privacy, Family, Home, or Correspondence

The law prohibits such actions, but authorities frequently interfered with the privacy of persons regarded as enemies of the government. There were reports security services monitored private e-mail and other digital correspondence.

The law provides for the interception of telephone calls with prior authorization from the prime minister at the request of the minister of interior or minister of defense.

Militias and non-Lebanese forces operating outside the area of central government authority also frequently violated citizens' privacy rights. Various nonstate actors, such as Hizballah, used informer networks and telephone monitoring to obtain information regarding their perceived adversaries.

LAF forces raiding Syrian refugee settlements caused destruction of physical property while making arrests.

Personal status was legally handled by religious courts, which applied religious laws of the various confessions and occasionally interfered in family matters such as child custody in the case of divorce. Refugee birth registrations require families to register birth certificates with Lebanese ministries, which remained inaccessible because the ministries require proof of legal residence and legal marriage.

g. Use of Excessive Force and Other Abuses in Internal Conflicts

Da'esh and other extremist groups conducted an offensive in the town of Arsal, a key refugee hub in the Bekaa Valley, in August 2014. To protect civilians, the army evacuated Arsal, resulting in the displacement of tens of thousands of citizens and Syrian refugees during the counteroffensive. Some displaced civilians received assistance from aid groups. The military closed the town for several days to human rights groups, limiting their ability to investigate the army's conduct.

Section 2. Respect for Civil Liberties, Including:

a. Freedom of Speech and Press

The law provides for freedom of speech and press and stipulates that restrictions may be imposed only under exceptional circumstances. The government generally respected these rights, but there were some restrictions, particularly regarding political and social issues.

Freedom of Speech: Individuals were free to criticize the government but were legally prohibited from publicly criticizing the president (a post which was vacant throughout the year) and foreign leaders. Authorities also hindered the expression of certain views.

Press and Media Freedoms: Independent media outlets were active and expressed a wide variety of views. The majority of outlets had political affiliations, which hampered their ability to operate freely in areas dominated by other political groups and affected their reporting. Local, sectarian, and foreign interest groups financed media outlets that reflected their views. The law restricts the freedom to issue, publish, and sell newspapers. Publishers must apply for and receive a license from the Ministry of Information in consultation with the press union.

The law governing audiovisual media bans live broadcasts of unauthorized political gatherings and certain religious events and prohibits the broadcast of "any matter of commentary seeking to affect directly or indirectly the well-being of the nation's economy and finances, material that is propagandistic and promotional, or promotes a relationship with Israel." Media outlets must receive a license from the Council of Ministers, based on a recommendation by the minister of information, to broadcast direct and indirect political news and programs. The law also prohibits broadcasting programs that seek to affect the general system, harm the state or its relations with Arab and other foreign countries, or have an effect on the well-being of such states. The law also prohibits the broadcast of programs that seek to harm public morals, ignite sectarian strife, or insult religious beliefs.

On September 18, the STL found Karma Khayat, the deputy chief executive officer and deputy news director of Al-Jadeed TV, guilty of contempt of court by ignoring a court order to remove broadcasts made in 2012 about purported confidential STL witnesses from the station's website. The STL acquitted Khayat of the more serious offence of intimidating witnesses. The station was acquitted of corporate liability on both counts. It was the first judgment handed down by the STL.

Violence and Harassment: On May 17, an unknown assailant beat Saida Net website journalist Hilal Hibli. An unknown person threatened journalist Dima Sadek's mother on May 15 after her daughter published a comment on her Facebook page criticizing the sentencing of former minister of information and U.S.-designated global terrorist Michel Samaha; Sadek was forced to delete the comment.

In civil society-led protests on August 22 and 23 against the government's handling of garbage collection services, security forces injured an estimated 10 journalists, hitting them with batons, throwing stones at them, and deliberately damaging their equipment. On September 20, politically affiliated gangs assaulted journalist Osama Kaderi of *Al-Akhbar* newspaper. The gangs reportedly objected to negative depictions of political leaders during the garbage protests in Beirut's Martyr's Square.

<u>Censorship or Content Restrictions</u>: The law permits, and authorities selectively used, prior censorship of pornographic material, political opinion, and religious material considered a threat to national security or offensive to the dignity of the head of state or foreign leaders. The DGS reviewed and censored all foreign newspapers, magazines, and books to determine admissibility into the country. Political violence and extralegal intimidation led to self-censorship among journalists.

The law includes guidelines regarding materials deemed unsuitable for publication in a book, newspaper, or magazine. Any violation of the guidelines could result in the author's imprisonment or a fine.

Authors could publish books without prior permission from the DGS, but if the book contained material that violated the law, the DGS could legally confiscate the book and put the author on trial. In some cases authorities might deem the offending material a threat to national security. Such offenses were not taken to trial based on the publication law, but rather on the basis of criminal law or other statutes. Publishing a book without prior approval and that contained unauthorized material could put the author at risk of a prison sentence, fine, and confiscation of the published materials.

Authorities of any of the recognized religious groups could request the DGS to ban a book. The government could prosecute offending journalists and publications in the publications court.

On January 14, the attorney general issued a search and investigation warrant against Syrian journalist Faisal El-Kassem, after he insulted the Lebanese army on social media. On January 19, the DGS censorship bureau banned the distribution of that day's editions of two French daily newspapers, *Le Monde* and *Liberation*, after they republished cartoons from the weekly French magazine *Charlie Hebdo* that the DGS deemed offensive to religions. On April 18, an ISF officer prevented Future TV correspondent Salman al-Andari from filming in front of Roumieh Prison, the site of prisoner abuse allegations. On September 1, riot police forcibly ejected journalists covering the antigarbage civil society protest movement's occupation of the Environment Ministry building, while clearing the building of protesters who blamed the minister for the crisis. Police officers hit journalists inside and outside the building and confiscated their equipment or rendered it inoperable.

Libel/Slander Laws: The 1991 security agreement between the Lebanese and Syrian governments, still in effect at year's end, contained a provision prohibiting the publication of any information deemed harmful to the security of either state.

In October authorities arrested a Palestinian woman for defamation against the army in accordance with article 403 of the penal code after she gave an interview alleging rape and torture at the hands of LAF officers in 2013. The woman was released on bail, and at year's end the investigative judge was determining whether to press charges in court.

Nongovernmental Impact: Radical Islamist groups sometimes sought to inhibit freedom of the press through coercion and threat of violence.

Internet Freedom

The law does not restrict access to the internet. There was a perception among knowledgeable sources, however, that the government monitored e-mail, Facebook, Twitter, blogs, and internet chat rooms where individuals and groups engaged in the expression of views. The government reportedly censored some websites to block online gambling, pornography, and religiously provocative material, but there were no verified reports the government systematically attempted to collect personally identifiable information via the internet. Digital activists circulated leaked correspondence among government institutions showing that intelligence agencies sought to purchase spyware.

In the absence of laws governing online media and activities on the internet, the ISF's Cyber Crimes Unit and other state agencies summoned journalists, bloggers, and activists to question them about tweets, Facebook posts, and blog posts critical of political figures.

Restrictions on freedom of speech concerning the president applied to social media communications on Facebook and Twitter, which authorities considered a form of publication rather than private correspondence. There were also reports of political groups intimidating individuals and activists for their online posts. In August an online campaign targeted activist and blogger Assaad Thebian, one of the main figures in the antigarbage, anticorruption civil society movement called "You Stink," over Facebook posts he had written in 2013 and 2014 about religious festivals. The online campaign, allegedly organized by the Free Patriotic Movement political party, accused Thebian of defaming religious rites through his social media postings; no action was taken following the initial accusations.

Internet access was available and widely used by the public. According to the
International Telecommunication Union, internet penetration was 74.7 percent in
2014.

Academic Freedom and Cultural Events

There are no government restrictions specific to academic freedom, but libel and
slander laws apply. The government censored films, plays, and other cultural
events. The DGS reviewed all films and plays and prohibited those deemed
offensive to religious or social sensibilities. DGS's decision-making process
lacked transparency and was influenced by the opinions of religious institutions
and political groups. Cultural figures and those involved in the arts practiced self-
censorship to avoid being detained or refused freedom of movement. On May 31,
during the Cabriolet short film festival, the DGS refused to grant the movie
Solitaire a screening permit. In January the NGO March said the censorship
bureau banned several of its play scripts; DGS stated it conditioned its approval to
changes to the texts.

b. Freedom of Peaceful Assembly and Association

Freedom of Assembly

The constitution provided for freedom of assembly with some conditions
established by law, but the government sometimes restricted this right. Organizers
are required to obtain a permit from the Interior Ministry three days prior to any
demonstration. In previous years the ministry sometimes did not grant permits to
groups that opposed government positions, but there were no known examples of
this restriction being applied during the year.

Security forces occasionally intervened to disperse demonstrations, usually when
clashes broke out between opposing protesters.

On August 19, police authorities clashed with civil society activists from the "You
Stink" movement who were protesting the government's paralysis over the
accumulation of trash in the streets, the government's discussion of allegedly
corrupt bids to solve the trash crisis, and the government's inability to resolve the
crisis. Security authorities used force to disperse the protesters; security forces
fired water hoses, and kicked and beat protesters with batons to stop them from
tearing down the barbed wire separating them from the parliament building.

Human rights NGOs reported that the police actions injured hundreds of citizens, and many demonstrators went to the hospital. The Ministry of Interior conducted an internal investigation into the use of violence and referred two ISF officers to the Disciplinary Council. Six officers faced disciplinary measures as a result of "an excessive use of force."

On September 16 and September 20, during additional antigarbage civil society demonstrations in Beirut, politically affiliated gangs attacked peaceful protesters for insulting political leaders by name.

Antigarbage protests continued on smaller scales throughout October, and from August to October many protesters were detained. Security forces ultimately released all demonstrators after their initial detention periods. The total number of protesters security forces detained and the number facing charges was unknown.

NGOs that advocated for women's rights, particularly those focused on combating domestic violence, organized protests and media campaigns that met with some interference by the security forces.

Freedom of Association

The constitution provides for freedom of association with some conditions established by law, and the government generally respected the law.

No prior authorization is required to form an association, but the Interior Ministry must be notified for it to be recognized as legal, and the ministry must verify that the organization respects public order, public morals, and state security. The ministry sometimes imposed additional inconsistent restrictions and requirements and withheld approval. In some cases the ministry sent notification of formation papers to the security forces to initiate inquiries on an organization's founding members. Organizations must invite ministry representatives to any general assembly where members vote on bylaws, amendments, or positions on the board of directors. The ministry must then validate the vote or election. Failure to do so may result in the dissolution of the organization by a decree issued by the Council of Ministers.

The cabinet must license all political parties (see section 3).

Independent NGOs in areas under Hizballah's sway faced harassment and intimidation, including social, political, and financial pressures. Hizballah reportedly paid youth who worked in "unacceptable" NGOs to leave the groups.

c. Freedom of Religion

See the Department of State's *International Religious Freedom Report* at www.state.gov/religiousfreedomreport/.

d. Freedom of Movement, Internally Displaced Persons, Protection of Refugees, and Stateless Persons

The law provides for freedom of internal movement, foreign travel, emigration, and repatriation, and the government generally respected these rights for citizens but placed extensive limitations on the rights of Palestinian refugees and during the year placed additional restrictions on Syrian refugees. As of November the Office of the UN High Commissioner for Refugees (UNHCR) registered 1,070,189 Syrian refugees. The UN Relief and Works Agency for Palestine Refugees in the Near East (UNRWA) provided assistance to Palestinian refugees registered in Lebanon (officially just under 450,000 individuals but estimated to be 300,000), as well as to those Palestinian refugees who were registered in Syria and who fled to Lebanon after 2011 and were recorded with UNRWA (approximately 42,000).

In-Country Movement: The government maintained security checkpoints, primarily in military and other restricted areas. Hizballah also maintained checkpoints in certain Shia-majority areas. Government forces were usually unable to enforce the law in the predominantly Hizballah-controlled southern suburbs of Beirut and did not typically enter Palestinian refugee camps. According to UNRWA, Palestinian refugees registered with the Interior Ministry's Directorate of Political and Refugee Affairs could travel from one area of the country to another. The directorate, however, had to approve the transfer of registration of residence for refugees who resided in camps. UNRWA stated the directorate generally approved such transfers. In 2012 authorities revoked the requirement to obtain an access permit to enter the Nahr el-Bared camp, and Lebanese and Palestinians entering the camps needed only to show their identity cards at LAF checkpoints outside the camp.

Under entry regulations that became effective in January, Syrian refugees registered with UNHCR must pay a renewal fee of 300,000 lira ($200) for each person age 15 or above for each additional 12 months the persons wishes to remain

in the country. In light of decreasing refugee resources, renewal fees were
prohibitive, and most refugees had difficulty affording the fees. Similarly, despite
DGS announcements that Palestinian refugees from Syria could renew their status
for three months upon payment of 300,000 Lebanese pounds ($200),
implementation was inconsistent and the cost prohibitively high for most of them.
In addition to the fee, refugees must provide legal housing documents, sign a
pledge not to work, and in some cases obtain a Lebanese sponsor. Due to these
regulations, many refugees were unable to renew their legal documents, which
significantly affected their freedom of movement owing to regular arrests at
checkpoints. By November the UN's joint household assessments of 100,000
families indicated that 87 percent refugee households had at least one member
without legal status. Refugees from Syria reported that if they were stopped at a
checkpoint and lacked valid visas or documents, they were often detained and sent
to the DGS detention center, a substandard facility located under a highway
overpass in Beirut. Authorities often held detainees for up to a week and required
them to pay high fines before releasing them.

Internally Displaced Persons

Fighting in 2007 destroyed the Nahr el-Bared camp, displacing 30,000 Palestinian
refugees. As of October, UNRWA reported that 9,247 Palestinian refugees
returned to housing units in Nahr el-Bared camp, while another 12,737 were living
in areas adjacent to the camp. The whereabouts of the remaining displaced
Palestinian refugees was not known.

Protection of Refugees

Access to Asylum: The law does not provide for the granting of asylum or refugee
status, and the country is not a party to either the 1951 convention relating to the
status of refugees or the 1967 protocol.

While 450,000 Palestinian refugees were officially registered with UNRWA, many
estimated the number to be less than 300,000 due to emigration. One-half of
refugees were under age 25, two-thirds lived below the poverty line, and one-third
suffered from chronic illness. Palestinian refugees were prohibited from accessing
public health and education services or owning land and were barred from
employment in many fields, making refugees dependent upon UNRWA as the sole
provider of education, health care, and social services. A 2010 labor law revision
expanded employment rights and removed some restrictions on Palestinian
refugees; however, this law was not fully implemented, and Palestinians remained

barred from working in most skilled professions, including almost all those that require membership in a professional association.

As of November 30, there were 1,070,189 Syrians registered with UNHCR, fleeing the civil war that broke out in 2011. There were no formal refugee camps in Lebanon for Syrians. Many Syrian refugees resided in temporary tent settlements, with host families, or in unfinished buildings. More than two-thirds of Syrian refugees in Lebanon lived in extreme poverty. A UN assessment of more than 4,000 refugee households found that an estimated 70 percent lived below the Lebanese extreme poverty line of $3.84 per day. According to the study, the refugees borrowed to cover even their most basic needs, including rent, food, and health care, putting nearly 90 percent of them in debt.

On January 5, new government regulations banned the entry of all Syrian refugees unless they qualified for undefined "humanitarian exceptions." UNHCR nevertheless continued to register Syrian refugees, and in the first quarter of the year registered 2,626 new arrivals who managed to enter after the cut-off date and 36,189 who were already in the country before the cut-off date. Accusing UNHCR of deception, the Ministry of Social Affairs on April 24 directed UNHCR to deregister the 2,626 new arrivals. On May 4, the ministry further directed UNHCR to cease all registrations, including registrations of those who had arrived before January 5, until a mechanism could be established to deal with "humanitarian exceptions." Due to the government's instruction to UNHCR to suspend registration as of May 6, there were no Syrians awaiting registration.

UNRWA reported that the DGS issued some Palestinian refugees from Syria departure orders despite having paid the renewal fee. Legal status in Lebanon was critical for protection from the authorities, as it ensured they could pass through checkpoints, including to and from camps, complete civil registration processes, and receive official exam results for students.

There was also a limited influx of Iraqi refugees who entered the country seeking to escape violence from the fight against Da'esh. As of November 28, there were 13,122 Iraqi refugees registered with UNHCR in Lebanon.

Refugee Abuse: Multiple NGOs and UNHCR shared reports of sexual harassment and exploitation by government employers and landlords of refugees, including paying workers below the minimum wage, working excessive hours, debt bondage, and pressuring families into early marriage for their daughters or nonconsensual sex.

The government lacked the capacity to provide adequate protection for refugees. Refugees regularly reported abuse by members of political parties and gangs, often without official action in response. Additionally, LAF raids on settlements often resulted in harassment and destruction of personal property.

According to UNHCR domestic courts often sentenced Iraqi and African refugees registered with UNHCR to one month's imprisonment and fines instead of deporting them for illegal entry. After serving their sentences, most refugees remained in detention unless they found employment sponsors and the DGS agreed to release them in coordination with UNHCR.

Employment: A pledge to not work is a requirement for Syrian refugees to obtain residency permits. Syrians who were not refugees were allowed to work, provided they had a sponsor for a work permit and could pay the associated fees.

A 2010 amendment to the social security law created a special account to provide end-of-service indemnities or severance pay to Palestinian refugees who retired or resigned. These benefits were available only to Palestinians working in the legal labor market. Palestinians did not benefit from national sickness and maternity funds or the family allowances fund. UNRWA continued to bear the cost of any medical, maternity, or family health-care expenses (excluding worker's compensation). The law provides for benefits only from 2010 onward.

Access to Basic Services: The government did not consider local integration of any refugees a viable, durable solution. After Syrians and Palestinians, Iraqis were the third-largest group of refugees in the country.

The law considers UNRWA-registered Palestinian refugees to be foreigners, and in several instances they received poorer treatment than other foreign nationals. UNRWA has the sole mandate to provide health, education, social services, and emergency assistance to the 450,000 registered Palestinian refugees residing in the country. The amount of land allocated to the 12 official Palestinian refugee camps in the country has changed only marginally since 1948, despite a four-fold increase in the population. Consequently, most Palestinian refugees lived in overpopulated camps, some of which were heavily damaged during past conflicts. In accordance with agreements with the government, Palestine Liberation Organization (PLO) security committees provided security for refugees in the camps, with the exception of the Nahr el-Bared camp. A comprehensive, multi-year plan to rebuild the Nahr el-Bared refugee camp and surrounding communities in eight stages began in 2008 and was in process, but remaining reconstruction was not fully funded, and only 60 percent of the required donations were secured by year's end.

A 2001 amendment to a 1969 decree barring persons who are explicitly excluded from resettling in the country from owning land and property was designed to exclude Palestinians from purchasing or inheriting property. Palestinians who owned property prior to the law entering into force were unable to bequeath it to their heirs, and individuals who were in the process of purchasing property in installments were unable to register the property.

Palestinian refugees residing in the country could not obtain citizenship and were not citizens of any other country. Palestinian refugee women married to Lebanese citizens were able to obtain citizenship and transmit citizenship to their children. Palestinian refugees, including children, had limited social and civil rights and no access to public health, education, or other social services. Children of Palestinian refugees faced discrimination in birth registration, and many had to leave school at an early age to earn an income.

Palestinians who fled Syria since 2011 received limited basic support from UNRWA, including food aid, cash assistance, and winter assistance. Authorities permitted their children to enroll in UNRWA schools and access UNRWA health clinics. As of November there were approximately 42,000 Palestinians refugees from Syria recorded with the agency.

The Ministry of Education and Higher Education facilitated the enrollment of more than 157,000 Syrian students in public schools in the 2015-16 academic year, and enrollment continued at year's end. Donor funding was available to support 200,000 children to enroll; however, the UN Children's Fund (UNICEF) estimated there were approximately 510,000 school-age Syrian refugee children. UN agencies covered school-related expenses, such as school fees, books, and uniforms. Syrian refugees had access to many government and private health centers and local clinics for primary care services, and UN agencies and NGOs funded the majority of associated costs. Syrian refugees had access to a limited number of UNHCR-contracted hospitals for emergency care.

Iraqi refugees had access to both the public and private education systems. UNHCR reported that 739 Iraqi children were registered in public schools, and it provided grants to the children's families to help defray the costs associated with attending school. Iraqi refugees also had access to the primary health-care system. UNHCR, through NGOs, provided secondary health care.

Temporary Protection: The government did not provide a temporary protection regime for asylum seekers, and it regularly deported refugees and asylum seekers who may have had valid claims to protected status. According to UNHCR, 331 refugees and asylum seekers were detained during the year, of whom 176 remained in detention as of October 15. During the year the DGS deported 15 persons despite UNHCR objections.

UNHCR continued to intervene with authorities to request the release of persons of concern who were detained either beyond their sentence or for illegal entry or presence.

Stateless Persons

Citizenship is derived exclusively from the father, resulting in statelessness for children of a citizen mother and a noncitizen father when registration under the father's nationality is not possible. This discrimination in the nationality law particularly affected Palestinians and increasingly Syrians from female-headed households. Additionally, some children born to Lebanese fathers may not have had their births registered due to a lack of understanding of the regulations or administrative obstacles. The problem was compounded since nonnational status was a hereditary circumstance that stateless persons pass to their children. There were no official statistics on the size of the stateless population.

Approximately 3,000 to 5,000 Palestinian refugees were not registered with UNRWA or the government. Also known as undocumented Palestinians, most of these individuals moved to the country after the expulsion of the PLO from Jordan in 1971. Palestinians faced restrictions on movement and lacked access to fundamental rights under the law. Undocumented Palestinians, who were not registered in other fields, were not necessarily eligible for the full range of services provided by UNRWA. Nonetheless, in most cases UNRWA provided primary health care, education, and vocational training services to undocumented Palestinians. The majority of undocumented Palestinians were men, many of them married to UNRWA-registered refugees or Lebanese citizen women, who could not transmit refugee status or citizenship to their husbands or children.

The Directorate of Political and Refugee Affairs continued to extend late registration to Palestinian refugee children under age 10. It previously was the directorate's policy to deny late birth registration to Palestinian refugee children who were above age two. Children between age 10 and 20 were registered only after the following were completed: a DNA test, an investigation by the DGS, and the approval of the directorate.

Approximately 1,000 to 1,500 of an estimated 100,000 Kurds living in the country lacked citizenship, despite decades of family presence in the country. Most were descendants of migrants and refugees who left Turkey and Syria during World War I but were denied citizenship to preserve the country's sectarian balance. The government issued a naturalization decree in 1994, but high costs and other obstacles prevented many individuals from acquiring official status. Some individuals who received official status had their citizenship revoked in 2011, as a result of a presidential decree. Others held an "ID under consideration" document without date or place of birth.

Stateless persons lacked official identity documents that would permit them to travel abroad and could face difficulties traveling internally, including detention for not carrying identity documents. They had limited access to the regular employment market and no access to many professions. Additionally, they could not access public schools or public health-care facilities, register marriages or births, and own or inherit property.

Section 3. Freedom to Participate in the Political Process

Although the law provides citizens the ability to choose their government in free and fair periodic elections based on universal and equal suffrage, lack of government control over parts of the country, defects in the electoral process, prolonged extension of parliament's mandate, and corruption in public office significantly restricted this ability. The president and parliament nominate the prime minister, who, with the president, chooses the cabinet.

Elections and Political Participation

Recent Elections: In 2013 parliament postponed legislative elections to November 2014 and later rescheduled them for June 2017. Observers concluded that the 2009 parliamentary elections were generally free and fair, with minor irregularities, such as instances of vote buying. The NGO Lebanese Transparency Association reported its monitors witnessed election fraud through cash donations on election day in many electoral districts.

Political Parties and Political Participation: All major political parties and numerous smaller ones were almost exclusively based on confessional affiliation, and parliamentary seats were allotted on a sectarian basis.

Participation of Women and Minorities: There were significant cultural barriers to women's participation in politics. Prior to 2004, no woman held a cabinet position, and there have been only four female ministers since then. During the year one woman served in the cabinet. Only four of 128 members of parliament were women, and all were close relatives of previous male members. With a few notable exceptions, leadership of political parties effectively excluded women, limiting their opportunities for high office.

Minorities participated in politics to some extent. Regardless of the number of its adherents, every government-recognized religion, except Coptic Christianity, Ismaili Islam, and Judaism, was allocated at least one seat in parliament. Three parliamentarians representing minorities (one Syriac Orthodox Christian and two Alawites) were elected in the 2009 elections. None of the minority parliamentarians were women. These groups also held high positions in government and the LAF. Since refugees are not citizens, they have no political rights. An estimated 17 Palestinian factions operated in the country, generally organized around prominent individuals. Most Palestinians lived in refugee camps that one or more factions controlled. Palestinian refugee leaders were not elected, but there were popular committees that met regularly with UNRWA and visitors.

Section 4. Corruption and Lack of Transparency in Government

Although the law provides criminal penalties for official corruption, the government did not implement the law effectively, and officials often engaged in corrupt practices with impunity and on a wide scale. Government security officials, agencies, and police were subject to laws against bribery and extortion. The lack of strong enforcement limited the laws' effectiveness.

Corruption: Observers widely considered government control of corruption to be poor. Types of corruption generally encountered included systemic patronage; judicial failures, especially in investigations of politically motivated killings; electoral fraud facilitated by the absence of preprinted ballots; and bribery. Bribes customarily accompanied bureaucratic transactions. In addition to regular fees, customers paid bribes for driver's licenses, car registrations, or residential building permits. Syrian refugees reportedly paid bribes to shopkeepers or municipal officials for a variety of services, for example, to receive consignment of aid or facilitate their registration.

Financial Disclosure: The law requires the president of the republic, the president of the Chamber of Deputies, and the president of the Council of Ministers to disclose their financial assets in a sealed envelope deposited at the Constitutional Council, but the information is not made available to the public. Judges disclose their financial assets in a sealed envelope at the Higher Judicial Council, and civil servants deposit their sealed envelopes at the Civil Servants Council, but the information is also not available to the public.

A 2011 report by the Lebanese Transparency Association claimed corruption was institutionalized. Since parliament had not passed a budget since 2005, there was limited parliamentary or auditing authority oversight of revenue collection and expenditures.

Public Access to Information: There were no laws regarding public access to government documents, and the government generally did not respond to requests for documents.

Section 5. Governmental Attitude Regarding International and Nongovernmental Investigation of Alleged Violations of Human Rights

A number of domestic and international human rights groups generally operated without government restriction, investigating and publishing their findings on human rights cases. Government officials generally were not responsive to these groups' views, and there was limited or no accountability for human rights violations.

Government Human Rights Bodies: The parliamentary Committee on Human Rights struggled to advance legislative proposals to make legal changes to guide ministries in protecting specific human rights or, for example, improving prison conditions. The Ministry of Interior had a human rights department to enhance and raise awareness about human right issues within the ISF, train police officers on human right standards, and monitor and improve prison conditions. The ministry staffed the department with two officers, two sergeants, and an information technology specialist, in addition to the department's head. The department was not adequately resourced. Its leadership maintained high standards of professionalism, but due to the integrated structure, the department's independence could not be assured.

In April 2014 the ISF launched a revised complaint mechanism allowing citizens to track complaints and receive notification of investigation results. Citizens may file formal complaints against any ISF officer in person at a police station, through a lawyer, by mail, or online through the redesigned ISF website. At the time a complaint is filed, the filer receives a tracking number that may be used to check the status of the complaint throughout the investigation. The complaint mechanism provides ISF the ability to notify those filing complaints of the results of its investigation.

The LAF has a human rights unit that engaged in human rights training through the Department of Defense's Defense Institute of International Legal Studies. The unit worked to ensure the LAF operates in accordance with major international human rights conventions.

Section 6. Discrimination, Societal Abuses, and Trafficking in Persons

The law provides for equality among all citizens and prohibits discrimination based on race, gender, disability, language, or social status. Although the government generally respected these provisions, they were not enforced, especially with regard to economic matters, and aspects of the law and traditional beliefs discriminated against women. The law does not protect against discrimination based on sexual orientation or gender identity.

Women

Rape and Domestic Violence: The law criminalizes rape. While the government effectively enforced the law, its interpretation by religious courts precluded full implementation of civil law in all provinces. Rape and domestic violence were underreported. The minimum prison sentence for a person convicted of rape is five years, or seven years for raping a minor. According to the penal code, the state would not prosecute a rapist and would nullify his conviction if the rapist married his victim. The law does not criminalize spousal rape. According to the domestic NGO KAFA (Enough Violence and Exploitation), 80 percent of domestic-violence victims the NGO assisted suffered spousal rape.

In April 2014 parliament passed legislation for the Protection of Women and Family Members from Domestic Violence. The law criminalizes domestic violence, but it does not specifically provide protection for women. The law does not criminalize spousal rape but rather the use of threats or violence to claim a

Country Reports on Human Rights Practices for 2015
United States Department of State • Bureau of Democracy, Human Rights and Labor

"marital right to intercourse," and it does not criminalize the nonconsensual violation of physical integrity. The maximum sentence under this law is 25 years' imprisonment if one of the spouses commits homicide.

A 2010 UN Population Fund assessment estimated there were high rates of domestic violence in the country. Despite a law that sets a maximum sentence of 10 years in prison for battery, some religious courts may legally require a battered wife to return to her home despite physical abuse. Foreign domestic workers, usually women, often were mistreated, abused, and in some cases raped or placed in slavery-like conditions (see section 7.c.). Some police, especially in rural areas, treated domestic violence as a social, rather than criminal, matter.

The government provided legal assistance to domestic violence victims who could not afford it, and police response to complaints submitted by battered or abused women improved. The NGOs Lebanese Council to Resist Violence against Women and KAFA offered counseling and legal aid and raised awareness about the problem. In 2014 KAFA assisted victims in 649 cases of violence, the majority of which concerned domestic violence.

Other Harmful Traditional Practices: In contrast with 2014, there were no reports of honor killings.

Sexual Harassment: The law prohibits sexual harassment, but authorities did not enforce the law effectively, and it remained a widespread problem. According to the UN Population Fund, the labor law does not explicitly prohibit sexual harassment in the workplace; it merely gives a male or female employee the right to resign without prior notice from his or her position in the event that an indecent offense is committed towards the employee or a family member by the employer or his or her representative, without any legal consequences for the perpetrator. Legal consequences are cited in the penal code and the criminal procedure.

Reproductive Rights: Couples and individuals have the right to decide the number, spacing, and timing of their children; manage their reproductive health; and have the information and means to do so, free from discrimination, coercion, or violence. Some women in rural areas faced social pressure on their reproductive choices due to long-held conservative values.

Discrimination: Women suffered discrimination under the law and in practice. Social pressure against women pursuing some careers was strong in some parts of society. Men sometimes exercised considerable control over female relatives, restricting their activities outside the home or their contact with friends and relatives. In matters of child custody, inheritance, and divorce, personal status laws provide unequal treatment across the various confessional court systems but generally discriminate against women. For example, Sunni civil courts applied an inheritance law that provides a son twice the inheritance of a daughter. Religious law on child custody matters favors the father in most instances. Nationality law also discriminates against women, who may not confer citizenship to their spouses and children, although widows may confer citizenship to their minor children. By law women may own property, but they often ceded control of it to male relatives due to cultural reasons and family pressure.

The law provides for equal pay for equal work for men and women, but in the private sector there was discrimination regarding the provision of benefits. Only 26 percent of women, compared with 76 percent of men, were in the formal labor force, and these women earned on average 61 percent of what men earned for comparable work (see section 7.d.).

The Women's Affairs Division in the Ministry of Social Affairs undertook some projects to address sexual or gender-based violence, such as providing counseling and shelter for victims and training ISF personnel to combat violence in prisons. In 2012 the government began commissioning women as ISF officers.

The National Commission for Lebanese Women, headed by the president's wife, is the highest governmental body addressing women's issues. Due to the continuing presidential vacancy, this post remained vacant.

Children

Birth Registration: Citizenship is derived exclusively from the father, which may result in statelessness for children of a citizen mother and noncitizen father who may not transmit his own citizenship (see section 2.d.). If a child's birth is not registered within the first year, the process for legitimating the birth is long and costly, often deterring families from registration. Syrian refugees faced numerous challenges registering their births because of the country's complicated registration system. Refugees without valid residency papers were not permitted to register their child's birth, preventing them from obtaining necessary documents for passports.

Some refugee children and the children of foreign domestic workers also faced obstacles to equal treatment under the law. NGOs reported discrimination against them, although some could attend public school.

Education: Education for citizens is free and compulsory through the primary phase. Noncitizen children, including those born of noncitizen fathers and citizen mothers and refugees, lack this right. Certain public schools had quotas for noncitizen children, but there were no special provisions for children of female citizens, and spaces remained subject to availability. Boys and girls had nearly equal rates of primary education, with women outnumbering men in secondary and tertiary education. Authorities permitted Syrian refugee children to enroll in public schools; however, the Ministry of Education limited enrollment to 100,000 Syrian students in public schools for the 2014-15 school year but aimed to reach 200,000 in the 2015-16 school year. UNICEF and the Ministry of Education and Higher Education learning program began during the year, enrolling nearly 7,000 students in catch-up classes to be grade-level ready for formal enrollment. Informal education was not recognized by the ministry, limiting the number of opportunities for refugee children to receive accredited education or a pathway to enroll once they achieved grade-level proficiency.

Child Abuse: According to a 2012 study by KAFA in partnership with the Ministry of Social Affairs, more than 885,000 children were victims of psychological abuse, of whom 738,000 were also victims of physical abuse and 219,000 were victims of sexual abuse. The Ministry of Social Affairs had a hotline to report cases of child abuse.

Syrian refugee children were vulnerable to child labor and exploitation.

Children reportedly joined local gangs engaged in sectarian violence in the northern part of the country.

Early and Forced Marriage: The legal age for marriage is 18 for men and 17 for women. Family matters are governed by confessionally determined personal status law, and minimum ages acceptable for marriage differ accordingly. UNHCR reported early and forced marriage was common in the Syrian refugee community. According to a study conducted by the Heartland Alliance in 2014, the marriages were not official but usually endorsed by sheikhs in the refugee community, often encouraged with a bribe. These sheikhs were not linked to the country's Sunni family courts, and the marriages had no legal standing.

Sexual Exploitation of Children: The penal code prohibits and punishes commercial sexual exploitation, child pornography, and forced prostitution. Prescribed punishment for commercial sexual exploitation of a person under age 21 is imprisonment for one month to one year and fines between 50,000 and 500,000 lira ($33 and $333). The maximum sentence for commercial sexual exploitation is two years' imprisonment. The minimum age for consensual sex is 18, and statutory rape penalties include hard labor for a minimum of five years and a minimum of seven years' imprisonment if the victim is younger than 15. Imprisonment ranges from two months to two years if the victim is between ages 15 and 18. The government generally enforced the law. As of September 30, the ISF investigated nine cases of human trafficking involving 11 victims of sexual exploitation and child trafficking and referred them to the judiciary. The DGS investigated 78 suspected cases of trafficking involving nonpayment of wages, physical abuse, and rape or sexual abuse. Many of the these cases were of children, although the statistics did not distinguish between child and adult victims. Additionally, the Ministry of Justice referred cases involving 89 suspected traffickers to the Public Prosecutor's Office, of which 72 individuals were charged under the antitrafficking law for alleged forced prostitution, forced labor, and forced child begging.

Displaced Children: The Ministry of Education and Higher Education opened 200,000 places in the public school system available to Syrian refugee children in the 2015-16 academic year. As of November, 157,000 Syrian refugee children had enrolled in public schools. NGOs often used informal education to assist students not performing at grade-level, but the ministry opposed nonformal education, which limited access to education for refugees and prompted many NGOs to terminate programs. UNICEF aimed to increase enrollment in accelerated learning programs to 90,000 in the 2015-16 academic year.

Some refugee children lived and worked on the street. Given the poor economic environment, limited freedom of movement and little opportunity for livelihoods for adults, many Syrian refugee families relied on children to be able to earn money for the family (see section 7.c.). Refugee children were at greater risk of exploitation and child labor, since they had greater freedom of movement compared to their parents, who often lacked residency permits.

International Child Abductions: The country is not a party to the 1980 Hague Convention on the Civil Aspects of International Child Abduction. For information see the Department of State's report on compliance at travel.state.gov/content/childabduction/en/legal/compliance.html and country-

specific information
at travel.state.gov/content/childabduction/en/country/lebanon.html.

Anti-Semitism

At year's end there were approximately 100 Jews living in the country and 6,000
registered Jewish voters who lived abroad but had the right to vote in
parliamentary elections.

The national school curriculum materials did not contain materials on the
Holocaust.

Trafficking in Persons

See the Department of State's *Trafficking in Persons Report*
at www.state.gov/j/tip/rls/tiprpt/.

Persons with Disabilities

Although prohibited by law, discrimination against persons with disabilities
continued. Employment law defines a "disability" as a physical, sight, hearing, or
mental disability. The law stipulates that at least 3 percent of all government and
private sector positions be filled by persons with disabilities, provided such
persons fulfill the qualifications for the position; however, no evidence indicated it
was enforced. Employers are legally exempt from penalties if they provide
evidence no otherwise qualified person with disabilities applied for employment
within three months of advertisement. The law mandates access to buildings by
persons with disabilities, but the government failed to amend building codes.
Many persons with mental disabilities received care in private institutions, several
of which the government subsidized (see section 7.d.).

The Ministry of Social Affairs and the National Council of Disabled is responsible
for protecting the rights of persons with disabilities. According to the president of
the Arab Organization of Disabled People, little progress had occurred since
parliament passed the law on disabilities in 2000. Approximately 100 relatively
active but poorly funded private organizations provided most of the assistance
received by persons with disabilities.

Depending on the type and nature of the disability, children with a disability may
attend mainstream school. Due to a lack of awareness or knowledge, school staff

often did not identify a specific disability in children and could not adequately advise parents. In such cases children often repeated classes or dropped out of school.

A 2002 Ministry of Education and Higher Education decree for new school building construction stipulates: "Schools should include all necessary facilities in order to receive the physically challenged." Nonetheless, the public school system was ill equipped to accommodate students with disabilities. Problems included a poor regulatory framework; poor infrastructure that was not accessible to persons with disabilities; curricula that did not include material to assist children with disabilities; laboratories and workshops that lacked the equipment required for children with disabilities; laboratories that lacked space and access for persons with disabilities, especially those using wheelchairs; teaching media and tools that relied increasingly on computers and audiovisual material that were not accessible to students with disabilities, including students who were blind, deaf, and those with physical disabilities; and lack of accessible transportation to and from schools.

Some NGOs (often managed by religious entities) offered education and health services for children with disabilities. The Ministry of Social Affairs contributed to the cost, although the ministry often delayed payments to the organizations. According to the ministry, it supported school attendance, vocational training, and rehabilitation for approximately 8,000 persons in 2014.

In the 2009 election, a Lebanese Physically Handicapped Union study showed only six of the country's 1,741 polling stations satisfied all criteria for accessibility.

National/Racial/Ethnic Minorities

A 2011 report funded by the EU and written by a coalition of local human rights organizations, *A Culture of Racism in Lebanon*, identified a widespread pattern of discrimination against persons who did not appear to be ethnically Lebanese. Lebanese of African descent attributed discrimination to the color of their skin and claimed harassment by police, who periodically demanded to see their papers. Foreign Arab, African, and Asian students, professionals, and tourists reported being denied access to bars, clubs, restaurants, and private beaches.

Syrian workers, usually employed as manual laborers and construction workers, continued to suffer discrimination, as they did following the 2005 withdrawal of Syrian forces from the country. Many municipalities enforced a curfew on

Syrians' movements in their neighborhoods in an effort to curb an increased number of robberies and to control security.

Acts of Violence, Discrimination, and Other Abuses Based on Sexual Orientation and Gender Identity

Official and societal discrimination against lesbian, gay, bisexual, and transgender (LGBTI) persons persisted. There is no all-encompassing antidiscrimination law to protect LGBTI persons. The law prohibits "unnatural sexual intercourse," an offense punishable by up to one year in prison but rarely applied; however, it often resulted in a fine. The Ministry of Justice did not keep records on these infractions. There were no reports authorities imprisoned anyone for violation of this law during the year.

Various NGOs, including Helem, AFE, and Marsa, hosted regular meetings in a safe house, provided counseling services, and carried out advocacy projects for the LGBTI community.

Information was not available on official or private discrimination in employment, occupation, housing, statelessness, or lack of access to education or health care based on sexual orientation or gender identity. The government did not collect such information, and individuals who faced problems were reluctant to report incidents due to fear of additional discrimination. There were no government efforts to address potential discrimination. During the year Marsa reported that a worker lost his job after informing the company's human resources department that he was HIV positive. During the year Oui Pour La Vie, an NGO working on the issue of stigma and discrimination against LGBTI persons, reported employers expelled two transgender women and one gay person from their work because of their gender identity and sexual orientation (see also section 7.d.).

NGOs claimed LGBTI persons underreported incidents of violence and abuse due to negative social stereotypes. Observers received reports from LGBTI refugees of physical abuse by local gangs, which the victims did not report to the ISF; observers referred victims to UNHCR-sponsored protective services.

Other Societal Violence or Discrimination

As in previous years, there were reports of incidents of societal violence and interreligious strife. Observers reported Shia militias, most notably Hizballah, harassed unfamiliar refugees entering territories under their control. The rise of

Da'esh, Nusra, and other extremist groups led to repeated fighting between the LAF and these groups. The same extremist groups also attacked Hizballah positions in the Bekaa Valley. Political leaders across the country condemned the action of extremist groups.

Section 7. Worker Rights

a. Freedom of Association and the Right to Collective Bargaining

The law provides for the right of private sector workers to form and join trade unions, strike, and bargain collectively but places a number of restrictions on these rights. The Ministry of Labor must approve the formation of unions, and it controlled the conduct of all trade union elections, including election dates, procedures, and ratification of results. The law permits the administrative dissolution of trade unions and bars trade unions from political activity. Unions have the right to strike after providing advance notice to and receiving approval from the local governor. Organizers of a strike (at least three of whom must be identified by name) must notify the governor of the number of participants in advance and the intended location of the strike, and 5 percent of a union's members must take responsibility for maintaining order during the strike.

There are significant restrictions on the right to strike. The law excludes public sector employees, domestic workers, and agricultural workers; therefore, they neither have the right to strike nor to join and establish unions. The law prohibits public sector employees from any kind of union activity, including striking, organizing collective petitions, or joining professional organizations. Despite this prohibition public sector employees succeeded in forming leagues of public school teachers and civil servants that created the Union of Coordination Committees (UCC), which along with private school teachers, demanded better pay.

The law protects the right of workers to bargain collectively, but a minimum of 60 percent of workers must agree on the goals beforehand. Collective bargaining agreements must be ratified by two-thirds of union members at a general assembly. The Union of Syndicates of Bank Employees and the Association of Banks renewed their collective agreement in 2013; the union requested to start negotiations to renew it. The union complained that many banks did not comply with the agreement. Employees of the Port of Beirut and the American University of Beirut Medical Center, among others, also had collective agreements with their employers.

The law prohibits antiunion discrimination. Under the law, when employers misuse or abuse their right to terminate a union member's contract, including for union activity, the worker is entitled to compensation and legal indemnity and may institute proceedings before a conciliation board. The board adjudicates the case, after which an employer may be compelled to reinstate the worker, although this protection was available only to the elected members of a union's board. Anecdotal evidence showed widespread antiunion discrimination, although this issue did not receive significant media coverage. Most flagrant abuses occurred in banking, private schools, retail businesses, daily and occasional workers, and the civil service. In August 2014 the Ministry of Education issued certificates of success for all students who had undergone official exams in an antiunion measure against teachers and the Union of Coordination Committee that continued to protest and demand improved conditions.

By law foreigners with legal resident status may join trade unions. The migrant law permits migrant workers to join existing unions (regardless of nationality and reciprocity agreements) but denies them the right to form their own unions. They do not enjoy full membership as they may neither vote in trade union elections nor run for union office. Certain sectors of migrant workers, such as migrant domestic workers, challenged the binding laws supported by some unions by forming their own autonomous structures that act as unions.

Palestinian refugees generally may organize their own unions on an ad hoc basis. Because of restrictions on their right to work, few refugees participated actively in trade unions. While some unions required citizenship, others were open to foreign nationals whose home countries had reciprocity agreements with Lebanon.

The government's enforcement of applicable laws was weak, including with regard to prohibitions on antiunion discrimination.

Freedom of association and the right to collective bargaining were not always respected. The government and other political actors interfered with the functioning of worker organizations, in particular the main federation, the General Confederation of Lebanese Workers (CGTL). The CGTL is the only national confederation recognized by the government, although several unions boycotted or unofficially or officially broke from the CGTL and no longer recognized it as an independent and nonpartisan representative of workers. The UCC, a grouping of public and private teachers as well as civil servants, largely overshadowed the CGTL, notably in pushing the government to pass a promised revised salary scale. Although UCC strikes and demonstrations prompted the government to send the revised salary scale proposal to parliament, parliament (which began meeting regularly again during the year) had yet to approve the proposal.

The law permits unions to conduct activities free from interference, but the Ministry of Labor interfered in union elections. Government officials and other political figures sought to influence union activities. In the past government officials encouraged the establishment of unions for political purposes to gain control of the CGTL.

Antiunion discrimination and other instances of employer interference in union functions occurred. Some employers fired workers in the process of forming a union before the union could be formally established and published in the official gazette.

Workers submitted a request to form the first domestic workers union in December 2014. The request was not recognized by year's end.

b. Prohibition of Forced or Compulsory Labor

The law prohibits all forms of forced or compulsory labor, but the government did not effectively enforce the law, although the government made some efforts to prevent or eliminate it.

Children, foreign workers employed as domestic workers, and other foreign workers sometimes worked under forced labor conditions. The law provides protection for domestic workers against forced labor, but domestic work is excluded from protections under the labor law and vulnerable to exploitation. In violation of the law, employment agencies and employers routinely withheld foreign workers' passports, especially in the case of domestic workers, sometimes for years. According to the Beirut Bar Association, authorities jailed one employer for a year for withholding an employee's passport. To mitigate this practice, the DGS began handing back passports to the worker rather than the employer. According to NGOs assisting migrant workers, some employers withheld salaries for the duration of the contract, which was usually two years.

Also see the Department of State's *Trafficking in Persons Report* at www.state.gov/j/tip/rls/tiprpt/.

c. Prohibition of Child Labor and Minimum Age for Employment

The minimum age for employment is 14, and the law prescribes the occupations that are legal for juveniles, defined as children between ages 14 and 18. The law requires juveniles to undergo a medical exam by a doctor certified by the Ministry of Public Health to assure they are physically fit for the type of work they are asked to perform. The law prohibits employment of juveniles for more than seven hours per day or from working between 7 p.m. and 7 a.m., and it requires one hour of rest for work lasting more than four hours. The law, updated by Decree 8987 on the Worst Forms of Child Labor, prohibits specific types of labor for juveniles, including informal "street labor." It also lists types of labor that, by their nature or the circumstances in which they are carried out, are likely to harm the health, safety, or morals of children under 16, as well as types of labor that are allowed for children over 16, provided they are offered full protection and adequate training.

The Ministry of Labor is responsible for enforcing child labor requirements through its Child Labor Unit. Additionally, the law charges the Ministry of Justice, the ISF, and the Higher Council for Childhood with enforcing laws related to child trafficking, including commercial sexual exploitation of children and the use of children in illicit activities. The HCC is also responsible for referring children held in protective custody to appropriate NGOs to find safe living arrangements. The Ministry of Labor employed approximately 90 labor inspectors, whom are also called upon to undertake child labor inspections. Overall, the government did not enforce child labor laws effectively, in part because of inadequate resources. The penalty is 50,000 lira ($33) per infraction. The penal code calls for penalties for those who abrogate child labor laws ranging from a fine of 250,000 lira ($165) to one- to three-months' imprisonment and closure of the offending establishment. Advocacy groups did not consider these punishments sufficient deterrents.

The government made efforts to prevent child labor and remove children from such labor during the year. Throughout the year the Ministry of Social Affairs and the HCC held awareness campaigns in schools and workshops for social workers who handle and journalists who cover child-related issues.

Child labor occurred, including in its worst forms. While up-to-date statistics on child labor were unavailable, anecdotal evidence suggested the number of child workers rose during the year and that more children worked in the informal sector, including commercial sexual exploitation, as UNHCR noted (see section 6, Children).

Child labor, including refugee children, was predominantly concentrated in the informal sector, including in small family enterprises, mechanical workshops, carpentry, construction, manufacturing, industrial sites, welding, agriculture including tobacco, and fisheries. Anecdotal evidence also suggested child labor was prevalent in Palestinian refugee camps and among Iraqi refugees and Romani communities, and most prevalent in the Syrian refugee community. Some children were involved in the worst forms of child labor, such as street work including begging, selling goods, polishing shoes, and washing car windows, as well as forced labor, sometimes as a result of human trafficking. The International Labor Organization noted abuses involving the use, recruitment, and exploitation of children in political protests and militant activities in North Lebanon and some areas of Beirut.

Also see the Department of Labor's *Findings on the Worst Forms of Child Labor* at www.dol.gov/ilab/reports/child-labor/findings/.

d. Discrimination with Respect to Employment or Occupation

The law provides for equality among all citizens and prohibits discrimination based on race, gender, disability, language, or social status. The law does not specifically provide for protection against discrimination based on sexual orientation, gender identity, HIV status, or other communicable diseases.

Although the government generally respected these provisions, they were not enforced, especially in economic matters, and aspects of the law and traditional beliefs discriminated against women. Discrimination in employment and occupation occurred with respect to women, persons with disabilities, foreign domestic workers, and LGBTI and HIV-positive persons (see section 6).

e. Acceptable Conditions of Work

The legal minimum wage, last raised in 2012, was 675,000 lira ($450) per month in the private sector.

The law prescribes a standard 48-hour workweek with a weekly rest period that must not be less than 36 consecutive hours. The law stipulates 48 hours work as the maximum per week in most corporations except agricultural enterprises. A 12-hour day is permitted under certain conditions, including a stipulation that overtime pay is 50 percent higher than pay for normal hours. The law does not set limits on compulsory overtime. The law includes specific occupational health and safety regulations and requires employers to take adequate precautions for employee safety.

Domestic workers are not covered under the labor law or other laws related to acceptable conditions of work. Such laws also do not apply to family concerns, day laborers, temporary workers in the public sector, or workers in the agricultural sector.

The Ministry of Labor is responsible for enforcing regulations related to acceptable conditions of work but did so unevenly. The ministry employed approximately 90 inspectors, made up of both inspectors and assistant inspectors, as well as administrators and technicians, who handle all inspections of potential labor violations. The number of inspectors, available resources, and legal provisions were not sufficient to deter violations, nor was the political will for proper inspections in other cases. Interference with inspectors affected the quality of inspections and issuance of fines for violators was common. The law stipulates that workers may remove themselves from situations that endanger their health or safety without jeopardy to their employment, although government officials do not protect employees who exercised this right.

Workers in the industrial sector worked an average of 35 hours per week, while workers in other sectors worked an average of 32 hours per week. Some private sector employers failed to provide employees with family and transportation allowances as stipulated under the law and did not register them with the National Social Security Fund (NSSF).

Some companies did not respect legal provisions governing occupational health and safety in specific sectors, such as the construction industry. Workers could report violations to the CGTL, Ministry of Labor, NSSF, or through their respective unions. In most cases they preferred to remain silent due to fear of arbitrary dismissal.

Violations of wage, overtime, and occupational health and safety standards were most common in the construction industry and among migrant workers, and particularly with foreign domestic workers.

Foreign migrant workers arrived in the country through local recruitment agencies and source-country recruitment agencies. Although the law requires recruitment agencies to have a license from the Ministry of Labor, the government did not adequately monitor their activities. A sponsorship system tied foreign workers' legal residency to a specific employer, making it difficult for foreign workers to change employers. If employment was terminated, a worker lost residency. This circumstance made many foreign migrant workers reluctant to file complaints to avoid losing their legal status.

There was no official minimum wage for domestic workers. Official contracts stipulated a wage ranging from 150,000 to 450,000 lira ($100 to $300) per month for domestic workers, depending on the nationality of the worker. A unified standard contract, which was registered with the DGS for the worker to obtain residency, granted migrant domestic workers some labor protections. The standard contract covered uniform terms and conditions of employment, but the section covering wages was completed individually.

Some employers mistreated, abused, and raped foreign domestic workers, who were mostly of Asian and African origin. Domestic workers often worked long hours and, in many cases, did not receive vacations or holidays. Victims of abuse may file civil suits or seek other legal action, often with the assistance of NGOs, but most victims, counseled by their embassies or consulates, settled for an administrative solution that usually included monetary compensation and repatriation.

Authorities did not prosecute perpetrators of abuses against foreign domestic workers for a number of reasons, including the victims' refusal to press charges and lack of evidence. Authorities settled an unknown number of other cases of nonpayment of wages through negotiation. According to source-country embassies and consulates, many workers did not report violations of their labor contracts until after they returned to their home countries, since they preferred not to stay in the country for a lengthy judicial process.

In 2012 Lebanese Broadcasting Corporation International television released a video by an anonymous bystander in which a labor recruiter, identified as Ali Mahfouz, physically abused Ethiopian domestic worker Alem Dechasa-Desisa outside the Ethiopian consulate in Beirut. Dechasa-Desisa subsequently committed suicide at the Deir el-Saleeb psychiatric hospital. Following the investigation the Beirut prosecutor general charged Mahfouz with contributing to and causing Dechasa-Desisa's suicide, and the case was referred to the Beirut penal court. By year's end, however, the Ministry of Labor had not reported any action against Mahfouz's labor agency.

While licensed businesses and factories strove to meet international standards for working conditions with respect to occupational safety and health, conditions in informal factories and businesses were poorly regulated and often did not meet these standards. The Ministry of Industry is responsible for enforcing regulations to improve safety in the workplace. The regulations require industries to have three types of insurance (fire, third-party, and workers policies) and to implement proper safety measures. The ministry has the authority to revoke a company's license if its inspectors find a company noncompliant.

The law requires businesses to adhere to safety standards, but it was poorly enforced and did not explicitly permit workers to remove themselves from dangerous conditions without jeopardy to their continued employment.

Brian D. Lerner is an Immigration Lawyer and runs a National Immigration Law Firm for nearly 30 years. He is an attorney who is a certified specialist that might help in Immigration & Nationality Law as issued by the California State Bar, Board of Legal Specialization. Attorney Lerner is an expert in Immigration Law, Removal and Deportation, Citizenship, Waiver and Appeals.

He has been a licensed attorney since 1992 and started the Law Offices of Brian D. Lerner, APC. The immigration practice consists of Immigration and Nationality Law, and everything involved with and regarding immigration which includes citizenship, investment visas, family and employment visas, removal and deportation hearings, appeals, waivers, adjustment, consulate processing and all types of immigration and citizenship matters.

He has represented clients from all over the U.S. and in many countries around the world. One side of his practice is dedicated to keeping people in the U.S. and fighting for their immigration rights, while another side is to get people back who have been deported and removed from the U.S.

Also, there is the affirmative part of Immigration Law which Brian Lerner has helped numerous people come into the U.S. on business visa, investment visas, student visas, fiancee and marriage visas, religious visas and many more. Attorney Lerner has helped immigrants who are victims of crime and domestic violence or ones that are married to abusers.

In other words, Attorney Lerner has a firm that helps people all over the U.S. He has dedicated significant time to preparing numerous petitions and applications for you to get at a fraction of the price of hiring an attorney. He says it is the next best thing to a real attorney because they are real petitions prepared by an expert.